D1552942

Capturing the Magic of Fiction Writing

Capturing the Magic of Fiction Writing

Jack Creed

Glenbridge Publishing Ltd.

Library of Congress Catalog Card Number: 90–80208

International Standard Book Number 0–944435–10–6

for Maria Christina Vasquez
for bringing so much love
into my life

Contents

Foreword

When the subject is fiction writing, I like to think of the story by Cervantes about the artist who was asked by a curious bystander what he was painting. "Whatever it turns out to be," the artist replied. That, of course, is not the way to approach painting, and it is also not the way to approach fiction writing.

Is the writing of fiction an art, a skill, or a craft? Can you be a "born writer," or can writing be learned? The answer, of course, is "yes" to all of the above. That you are reading this book sets you apart, and on a very promising note. You have acted on the impulse to write. That simple step is one that many would-be writers never take, and yet it is crucial. Who knows? There are undoubtedly many potentially great writers out there now with the innate art and ability to produce magnificent works of fiction, but the world will never know of them because they have not acted on the impulse.

You have chosen wisely. As one of those fortunate enough to be using this book, you will find the way considerably enhanced for you as a writer. A particular strength that Jack

Creed brings to this text is his organizational skill. Unlike other volumes that tend to become so technical as to appear dry and mechanical, or others that are given to esoteric values that they never quite make that magic landing into reality, this book will take you on an enjoyable, clearly-marked pathway to effective fiction writing that is enriched throughout with excellent examples from great writers and great writing.

You will find two good reasons for using this book. One is the outstanding clarity with which the author provides down-to-earth advice, the realistic guidelines for you to follow in becoming a knowledgeable and conscious artist. Second is the rich and compelling selection of examples from known literature and the original writing samples provided by the author to illustrate not only what effective fiction writing is but also what it sometimes is not. Those examples alone make this book worthwhile, for it is in them that so many of the richest lessons in fiction writing can be learned.

Step by interesting step, Jack Creed covers every magic step of fiction writing in this book, and along the way will make you richly aware of what is involved in becoming the best writer of which you are capable. Before you lies some of the best advice you can ever find on both the art and the craft of fiction writing. You will be pleased to discover from the earliest pages that the essence of writing is tied directly to—you.

Dr. Tom Parks, Associate Professor
of Education and Director, Office of
Extension and Public Relations,
Clemson University

Preface

A thorough analysis of prose fiction genres is a formidable undertaking, whether you're a college student facing tough courses in literature and composition or an aspiring writer longing to capture a large readership. How much more utterly impossible it must seem, then, for the bright high school student who enters college and discovers he is not prepared for the great leap into the broad spectrum of structures, critical elements, and writer techniques that must be identified and analyzed effectively.

Everyone has valid and often critical reasons for studying the exciting intricacies of prose fiction. Perhaps your high school preparations for critical analyses are inadequate for the high standards set by our colleges and universities. On the other hand, perhaps your studies have merely piqued your appetite for discovering more about the craft of writing and for becoming published yourself. Perhaps the smell of printer's ink and the onset of writer's-bug-fever have exacted a heavy toll on your time and energy, but you have only reams of scribblings and doodlings to show for it. False starts, flat middles, and pointless endings have led you to an important discovery: The magic for creating original fiction is often painfully elusive.

Capturing the Magic of Fiction Writing was developed to provide aspiring writers as well as teachers and students of literature and composition a practical guide to ease the transition from analyzing the basic story into discovering and applying the essential tools of the writer's craft. The structure of the book is in three essential parts: Part 1, "Examining the Target," explains the importance of organization and discipline to successful writing, defines the terms encountered in the studies of prose fiction, and demonstrates the relationships of these terms to the structures of prose fiction genres. All key fiction elements are introduced, defined, and explained or illustrated with writing samples. In addition, eight supportive elements are introduced, providing a broader base for student discovery, for story analyses, and for actual writing applications.

Part 2, "Analyses of Fiction Elements and Techniques," presents each of the six key elements in separate chapters, elaborating fully upon their purposes, structures, and applications in both short stories and novels. Here, you begin to perceive the techniques for creating these elements, for they are amply illustrated in writing samples.

Finally, Part 3, "Analyses of Supportive Elements and Techniques," expands upon the initial introduction of supportive elements, again providing explanations and writing samples to help you perceive the techniques presented. From these practical illustrations, you will learn to recognize, define, interpret, select, organize, and apply those supportive elements that work best for your personal objectives.

The presentation of the book is unique in several ways. Here you will find a unified, coherent organization of essential writing elements and techniques; a practical, thorough exploration of writing samples that illustrate essential writing strategies; an effective sampling of professional references; an extensive examination of symbols, symbolic plants, and the symbolic reference too often passed over quickly or ignored by many authorities.

Much of the technical language is made simpler by repeated references to prose fiction elements and techniques, first in the introductory chapters and afterwards in the expanded coverage. Each repetition allows you to grasp the full relationships of writing terms and encourages you to apply these in your discussions and in your own writing.

High school English teachers will find the book particularly beneficial, especially those teachers who have had little or no preparation for teaching creative writing courses. Here is the information you need to teach your gifted students the essential concepts of story analysis and composition. In addition, your student journalists will quickly learn how to use their knowledge of fictional elements and creative writing techniques in structuring news articles and critical essays and in writing authoritative book reviews for local newspapers and magazines.

Capturing the Magic of Fiction Writing is an appropriate supplementary text for college-level creative writing instructors and students, for teachers and students of advanced studies in literature and composition, and, as a practical trade reference, for aspiring writers. It is, as well, a most effective reference for all school and public libraries.

Acknowledgments

Grateful acknowledgment is made to the following for their permissions to reprint brief excerpts from copyrighted materials:

The Atlantic Monthly and James Hurst for permissions to reprint an excerpt from "The Scarlet Ibis," by James Hurst. Copyright © 1960 by James Hurst; published by *The Atlantic Monthly,* June 1960.

Bantam Books for permission to reprint an excerpt from *The Last of the Breed,* by Louis L'Amour. Copyright © 1986 by Louis L'Amour; published by Bantam Books, 1986.

Brandt and Brandt for permission to reprint excerpts from *The Big Gamble,* by George Harmon Coxe. Copyright © 1958 by George Harmon Coxe; published by Alfred A. Knopf, Inc., 1958.

Doubleday & Company and Stephen King for permission to reprint an excerpt from *Pet Sematery,* by Stephen King. Copyright © 1983 by Stephen King; published by Doubleday & Company, a division of Bantam, Doubleday, Dell Publishing group, 1983.

Marjorie Franco for permission to reprint excerpts from "Chance Of A Lifetime," by Marjorie Franco. Copyright © 1989 by Marjorie Franco; published in *Redbook,* March 1989.

Harper & Row Publishers for permission to reprint brief excerpts from *The Thornbirds,* by Colleen McCullough. Copyright © 1977 by Colleen McCullough; published by Harper & Row Publishers, 1977.

Ann Hood for permission to reprint excerpts from "Fanning An Old Flame," by Ann Hood. Copyright © 1989 by Ann Hood; published in *Redbook,* March 1989.

Alfred A. Knopf for permission to reprint excerpts from "Miss Brill," by Katherine Mansfield, from *The Short Stories of Katherine Mansfield.* Copyright © 1922, 1927 by Alfred A. Knopf, and renewed by John Middleton Murry.

Alfred A. Knopf for permission to reprint brief excerpts from *The Light in the Forest,* by Conrad Richter. Copyright © 1953 by Conrad Richter; published by Alfred A. Knopf, 1953.

MacDonald & Co., Ltd. for permission to reprint excerpts from *The Thornbirds,* by Colleen McCullough. Copyright © 1977 by Colleen McCullough; published by Harper & Row Publishers, Inc. 1977.

Harold Matson Company, Inc. for permission to use brief excerpts from "The Restless Ones," by Leslie Waller. Copyright © 1954 by Leslie Waller.

Penguin Books USA, Inc. for permission to use a brief excerpt from *The Grapes of Wrath,* by John Steinbeck. Copyright © 1939 by John Steinbeck; copyright © renewed by John Steinbeck, 1967; Penguin paperback edition, 1981.

Mayer, Brown & Platt and The Hemingway Foreign Rights Trust for permission to reprint excerpts from "Hills Like White Elephants," from *Men Without Women,* by Ernest Hemingway. Copyright © 1927 by Charles Scribner's Sons, an imprint of Macmillan Publishing Company; renewal copyright © 1955 by Ernest Hemingway.

G. P. Putnam's Publishing Group for permission to use an excerpt from *The Last Convertible,* by Anton Myrer. Copyright © 1978 by Anton Myrer; published by G. P. Putnam's Sons, 1978.

Charles Scribner's Sons, an imprint of Macmillan Publishing Company, for permission to print excerpts from "Hills Like White Elephants," from *Men Without Women,* by Ernest Hemingway. Copyright © 1927 by Charles Scribner's Sons; renewal copyright © 1955 by Ernest Hemingway.

The author wishes to express his appreciation for the generous support and/or helpful suggestions given by Mark Breger, former English teacher at Midland Valley High School, for listening to my plans for this project and cffering suggestions and the encouragement I needed during the early stages of writing the book; Nellie Elam Smith, library media specialist at Midland Valley High School for her generous help; the following librarians at Aiken County Library for their generous assistance; Sally Farris, head librarian, Ermma Gray, circulation manager, Fay Verburg, reference librarian, and Lorraine Sanders, circulation desk clerk; Rev. Ray F. Kneece, poet and essayist, for contributing his knowledge of word processing; L. Troy Nobles, Director of Administration and Operations, Area 1, Aiken County Schools, for his kindness and generous help; Nila J. Beard, Coordinator, Aiken County Teacher Incentive Programs, for sharing my excitement for the book; Jane McGraw, copy editor, for her splendid editing and suggestions for revisions; and James A. Keene, my editor, for his guidance and support in all stages of the project; all have made the task of bringing the book together an exciting adventure.

Part One
Examining the Target

1

Where Is the Magic?

The writer's bug is a formidable creature whose bite produces a feverish enthusiasm for writing that lasts for variable periods of time. Thousands of its victims have been bewitched and forced to sit for long hours, day or night, creating fictional characters and plots, many of which have brought goose pimples to our flesh and tears to our eyes. When we compare the writings of successful authors, we discover that each story has its own distinct charm, that it stands as a unique blend of that ever-elusive figment known as writer's magic. This blend is often drawn from contrasting story patterns, effects, and writing styles. Yet, in each selection, you and I are able to identify with the fictional characters and events and are left feeling satisfied with the story and its conclusion.

For many writers, however, aspirations rise and fall in irregular patterns as they become easily sidetracked by repeated failures or other interests, and eventually, little serious writing is attempted. These writers' hopes may be rekindled after reading an especially fine story which, of course, they could have written themselves if they'd only had the time. Rarely do aspiring authors admit that writing well-crafted stories has become a tedious chore.

Writing Is Hard Work

Writing publishable fiction is hard work, and even the serious student, one who is aware of the intricacies of plotting, dressing, and shaping an original effort, will sometimes face what look like insurmountable problems. When such moments occur, your prior devotion to learning your craft will provide the confidence and knowledge you need to overcome these difficulties. If you take the time to learn and apply the appropriate tools, you'll find that your efforts will be more exciting and worthwhile.

Many aspirants do manage to stay on track, maintaining a tenacious attitude in spite of repeated failures. Through trial and error, they begin to uncover the magic elements and techniques for shaping their own stories and for eventually getting them published. They come to know the thrill of receiving regular checks in their mailboxes and of seeing their names and titles in print. Through perseverance, they have captured the elusive magic of fiction writing.

First Sources of Magic

The beginning writer often acquires the first important bits of magic when he develops and maintains a keen sense of direction, follows up on his ideas with a detailed writing plan, and shows his willingness to study, write, and revise until the story is ready for the market. Writing about what is most interesting to you will help you over the snags and pitfalls that lie astride the path of every writer. Your enthusiasm for your plot and the characters who live it will supply you with those little sparks of energy you need to fire your imagination and drive you toward the finish.

Many surprises are in store for the beginner who writes and rewrites often, for the mind responds to a good workout. You'll be amazed at the professional elements that have crept in between the lines or emerged in the setting, dialogue, and action.

Magic in a Distinctive Style

How you choose to tell your story involves elements of viewpoint, transition, exposition, and narrative techniques, such as the use of dialogues, flashbacks, foreshadowing, narrative hooks, and symbols. The choices you make in expression, however, make up your writing style. If you have already written several short stories, or perhaps a novel, you will have discovered that your ideas have begun to flow more smoothly, revealing a distinct rhythm of words and phrases that are easy to read aloud without tripping over the tongue. Sentence and paragraph lengths vary, and sentence openers provide additional transitions of time, place, and importance to provide readers with visual images of setting and action.

To erase the rigidity of style sorely apparent in first writing efforts, set a length of time every day, at least five or more minutes for writing about any subject that comes to mind. If ideas stop flowing on one subject, begin another. Don't stop writing before the time is up! Also, don't stop to make corrections of any kind. With this activity, you are establishing mental discipline, teaching your mind to respond to a visual image of words, pictures, and any thoughts that occur during the writing process. Do this activity every day, looking back each time to examine what you have written and to note how you chose to express it.

Those first efforts will appear clumsy and contrived. Most of your sentences might begin with the subject, or perhaps you have deliberately introduced sentence openers of every kind. You will uncover favorite words that have been repeated too often. Some of your efforts might make little sense because the details are disorganized and show little depth of thought or completion. But if you make a habit of completing at least one timed writing exercise a day, you will develop confidence in your ability to say what you want to say in a style all your own.

Writing magic, then, is closely aligned with the organization of your study and writing time so that you can't say, "I don't have the time or a place for writing." Once you have set the time and place to write and study, hold on to these with the determination of a mountain lion. Friends will understand your need for periods of isolation and quiet when they observe how important your writing has become.

The Magic of Words

Writing magic is generated by your curiosity about new words. Begin using new words in your conversations and in your writings. Become more selective in your choices of words, using those that say exactly what you want to say. Use vivid words to describe faces in the crowd, to reveal emotions, actions, sounds, scents, tastes, and settings that will be strong images for readers.

Read More!

Well-read writers produce informed and exciting fiction. You will want to read on many subjects, including both fiction and nonfiction genres, for you want to acquire a richer vocabulary and a greater understanding of people, of the world, of ideas, and of yourself.

The more we read about others and their problems, the easier it becomes for us to recognize ourselves and our own problems. We begin to understand why we feel the way we do about so many things. We begin thinking about people we know and those we care about.[1] Finally, we begin to see how professional writers are able to make us recognize ourselves or others in the thoughts and experiences of fictional characters. Somehow they make us feel as though we are inside the scene and observing everything that is taking place, bystanders emotionally charged by our concern for fictional people. Some characters are despicable, and others are charming and lovable. When these two types appear in the same scene, we instantly take sides. Why? And how do writers keep us reading when television is seldom farther from us than the next room?

To find answers to these questions, you must read hundreds of stories like those you want to write. Learn to break them down into simple outlines that reveal the pattern the author used and the techniques he drew upon to grab your interest and maintain it. In such fashion, you will learn to plot a story before you write it, choosing characters we will love and hate, and to create credible situations we can readily identify with.

A Success Story

Erskine Caldwell, son of a Presbyterian minister, wrote book reviews before he became a published author of short stories and other genres of fiction and nonfiction. Through close analyses of the contents of the books he reviewed, Caldwell learned a variety of techniques for developing his own stories. But he did not mimic his teachers; fortunately, he recognized that to become a successful author, he would have to create story patterns and a style that were fresh and original.

Caldwell realized that success would not come easily. He struggled hard, as most writers do, often running short of money. But the desire to become a published author grew and took command of his efforts. He continued writing book reviews while practicing those techniques he would need to construct and market his own stories. He collected the books he received as payment for writing the reviews and began selling them to help pay expenses while he wrote. This money helped him carry out an important promise he had made to himself: He would isolate himself in the backwoods of Maine and not come out until he had sold a story.

Some months later, he submitted several short stories to Max Perkins, at that time an editor at Scribners. Shortly afterwards, he received a telephone call from the editor, who was interested in the stories.

"For how much?" the author asked.

"Three hundred dollars."

Caldwell was jubilant. He could now leave the backwoods life behind him. But when Max Perkins went on to explain that he was sending him three hundred dollars for each of the six stories he had submitted, Caldwell became downright ecstatic!

Erskine Caldwell had set a direction for himself and had persevered in developing strong, earthy characters who played out their roles in humorous and sometimes tragic settings in the South during the depression. His most successful novels are *Tobacco Road,* which was almost immediately adapted for stage and film, and *God's Little Acre,* also adapted for the silver screen. In addition, he wrote and published several highly readable collections of short stories, all rich in character and atmosphere.

Developing Your Craft

Writing fiction is a special craft, just as much as carpentry and crocheting are. Each has its own unique standards, tools, designs, and vocabulary for learning and creating their respective products. But knowing every tool, learning every unique term, and recognizing all techniques in fiction will not make you a writer. Writing professionally requires knowledge, discipline, perseverance, and a creative and imaginative inner spirit. That spirit thrives best when we use our senses to their fullest, collecting and absorbing details from our daily experiences and keeping a journal of events taking place around us. Ideas emerge from these notations, many of which often spark the imagination, and, thus, a story.

Your determination, consistent application of skills, and willingness to write and rewrite as often as necessary will eventually lead you to your own fictional magic, the most sought-after prize of every writer, beginner and professional alike. Set your own directions, identify your priorities, read and study what is being published, and write every day. The writers' marketplace is pulsing with variety and originality. There is always room for the beginner who has captured that elusive magic.

2

A First Step: Prose Fiction Terminology

Before you can be sure that you have written your stories in the most appropriate fashion (in other words, before you can be an effective self-critic), you must first become an efficient story analyst. To become a critical analyst, you will need to read and study fiction more carefully than the average reader. Much more. You must be able to discern the significance of even the smallest details, some that are concealed to all but the most critical eyes.

The first step in story analysis is to understand the unique positions of fiction, fictional genres, and fictional categories in the general frame of literature. Your understanding of these basic units will allow you to make accurate critical comparisons or to identify the contrasting elements and techniques that writers use to tell their stories.

Classifications in Literature

All forms of literature are grouped under two large umbrellas: fiction and nonfiction.

Fiction includes any story imagined by the author. The characters are not actual people, and the events did not take place exactly as presented. Of course, the characters might look and act like people you know in real life, for the writers have studied life and have created these original characters from composite descriptions of many people.

Writers choose their characters' traits to fit into particular situations, and they are chosen very carefully. No single character trait is original, for probably millions of people have that same trait. Some of these people have even been involved in a situation similar to the fictional incident.

Sometimes authors intentionally draw upon real-life characters and experiences. Thomas Wolfe, a realist from North Carolina, drew upon autobiographical situations from his childhood and from college for at least two of his novels, *The Web and the Rock* and *Look Homeward Angel.*[1]

Beginners, though, should strive to fictionalize their writings. Use fictitious names and settings and draw composites of several people you know for your plots and characterizations. Don't risk being sued for violations of the right to privacy by friends, relatives, or others.

Nonfiction includes all writings that report, analyze, teach, or entertain us by describing or predicting actual events and by portraying living or historical people. Examples of nonfiction writings include magazine articles, biographies, essays, historical studies, and most poetry, for a poem, like the stage or screen play, could be either fiction or nonfiction.

Fictional and Nonfictional Genres

Genres are specific forms of both fiction and nonfiction. You already recognize the differences between a printed page of prose and one of drama or poetry. These differences, and others not quite as obvious, allow us to group similar genres under a specific classification like prose fiction.

Prose fiction is a specific class of fiction comprised of two genres: short stories and novels. Other *fictional genres* are: (1) dramas (radio, stage, and TV); (2) fables; (3) legends; (4) monologues; and (5) myths.

Examples of *nonfictional genres* include letters, speeches, poetry, interviews, essays, biographies, autobiographies, articles, reviews, diaries, reports, and commentaries.

Fictional and Nonfictional Categories

Each fictional and nonfictional genre has a large number of categories. *Categories* are specific areas of reading interest found among book and magazine buyers. The market for novels and collections of short stories consists of faithful readers who keep demanding more of the same.

Here are some popular categories among the prose fiction genres:

GENERAL CLASSIFICATION: FICTION
Specific Classification: Prose Fiction
Genres: Short Stories and Novels

Categories			
western	satire	propaganda	espionage
adventure	gothic	supernatural	science fiction
mystery	spy	religion	human interests
humor	war	young adult	juveniles
romance	horror	nature	family crises

Classes of Novels

Novels are grouped under two general headings: category and mainstream.

The *category novel* is developed within the guidelines established by editors, writers, and publishers, who are aiming for special interest markets. For example, a gothic romance's length and plot are the major concerns of every publisher in this category. The market is studied regularly to monitor changes in readers' tastes, for these do occur periodically. Guidelines are rewritten to pamper the readers, and writers are quick to respond.

Upon close examination, you will uncover several writing formulas unique to each form of category novel. The illustrations alone on the book jackets of gothic romances tell us what is important for this category—the frightened heroine fleeing under gloomy skies, a tree bending in the wind; or perhaps she is standing on the moor with a cold, forbidding castle nearby.

Writers capitalize upon what has been successful and are careful to follow that formula for success. Quite often, a writer will produce stories that combine two or more categories. The combination increases the size of the market and usually results in larger sales. Several examples of category combinations are western-historical romance, fantasy-adventure, fantasy-satire, espionage-romance, ethnic-propaganda, ethnic-juvenile, teen romance-humor, detective-romance, teen romance-problem, space-war, and family crises-horror.

Mainstream novels interest buyers of practically every category taste. Their themes are drawn from topics of universal interest: rape, incest, political corruption, drug addiction, and other abuses that people inflict upon each other. On the positive side are stories that move from rags to riches, sin to salvation, or war to peace. These books are written to please universal audiences. Readers often pay higher prices for the usually heavier, more expensive volumes. Occasionally a mainstream blockbuster like *Love Story,* in spite of its short length and simple plot, will eventually sell millions of copies in hardcover and paperback editions.

It was not by accident that James Clavell's *Shogun,* an historical adventure, rose to the top of the best-seller lists. This two-volume novel embroiders a complex tale of bold adventurers caught up in the designs of Portuguese priests. Portugal's foothold in seventeenth-century Japan opened the door for her early trade supremacy there. Vivid descriptions of unrest among feudal lords, shaky alliances, and of three-dimensional, gutsy characters were fitting ingredients for a successful mainstream novel.

The Short Story

What is a *short story?* Obviously, a story that is short, but how much is short? Magazine guidelines list requirements of from 1,000 to 10,000 words. The smaller stories—between 1,000 to 1,800 words, give or take 200 words—are called short-shorts. The guidelines published in the current *Writer's Market* list 2,000 to 3,500 words as a popular range for many magazines. Longer pieces, especially those patterned in more than a single episode and ranging from 10,000 to 20,000 words, become novelettes or serialized versions of full-length novels.

Edgar Allen Poe gave us his definition of the short story in his famous review of Hawthorne's *Twice Told Tales* in 1842. He established the following principles, paraphrased here:

1. The short story must be short enough to be read in one brief sitting.

2. The story must create one impression.

3. Every word must be essential in producing that single effect.

4. The effect must be created in the initial sentence and developed throughout the story.

5. The number of characters is limited to those needed to produce the single effect.

6. When the story has reached the climax, the resolution comes quickly.

Additional story patterns have appeared since Poe's time, but insistence upon a single effect, few characters, and a short length continues to guide the work of most writers of this genre.

What Is a Novel?

Novels include prose fiction elements found in short stories, but their structure—if for no other reason than that they are longer—may contain considerably more complex plot patterns. Dick Perry, author of *One Way To Write Your Novel,* offers some insights into how writers might approach the craft of writing novels:

1. Novels of value offer useful ideas about life and present us with messages.

2. Messages of value must originate in the writer's heart.

3. The writer must accept that he will not please everyone with his work. Some readers will be shocked or confused, while others will be bored.

4. The writer must first be himself.

5. The writer must not be curbed by what "Uncle Fuddles" would want him to include in his novel. He will write the book he must write.

Perry also reminds us that a phony novel will never be published. "If you have a loudmouth who inside is tender, what do you care what the other loudmouths think? Write a tender novel. Other people—somewhere—are tender, too. They'll understand."[2]

Lawrence Block, a regular contributor to *Writer's Digest* and the author of more than one hundred books, has given beginners some solid insights about choosing the right genre for their first efforts. With a short story, Block can hold the entire plot in his head before he even begins typing. He writes the story out as it flows from his head. He knows where he's going, from start to finish. In writing the novel, few have that kind of grasp.[3] Instead, we keep surprising ourselves as characters become real-life people. The characters seem to be shaping themselves. The dialogues appear with little effort; new ideas generate other ideas that stimulate the next, and so on.[4]

A novel is not written all at once. You write it the way you live—one day at a time. All you need to know beforehand is what direction to take for that single day's writing.[5]

Escape Versus Quality Fiction

Your interests, attitudes, and objectives affect your purposes for reading or writing and govern the choices you make in approaching story analysis. It is a simple matter, therefore, to determine which class or classes of readers will be interested in any given genre: (1) readers who read for entertainment; or (2) readers who read to expand their awareness of life.[6]

Most fiction titles published today are aimed at the escape market, at readers who want to be entertained. These readers continue to demand formula stories and are likely to be readers of a single category. They choose stories that bring them emotional highs and that bring them down to earth again, delighted with the "happy ever after" conclusions. In *quality stories,* readers find pleasure in becoming engrossed in the treatment of current problems from the real world. Such stories leave readers with much for them to interpret for themselves.[7]

3

Three Classes of Prose Fiction

Mainstream novels differ significantly in their treatment of character, descriptive detail, and atmosphere. Category novels tend to rely upon those techniques that have proven successful in the past. Yet, both mainstream and category novels will be identifiable as one of three classes of prose fiction: (1) romance, (2) realism, or (3) naturalism.

Romance

Romance offers the reader an escape from reality. Novels of this class may take us to far-off places we often sit and dream about visiting. At the same time, we find ourselves drawn into another time; and, if we have learned our history and geography, we are able to fantasize further, capturing the high levels of physical and psychological imagery in setting and plot.

Usually the story is told from the heroine's point-of-view, a practical choice, since the majority of this category's authors and readers are women. Anne Gisconny, editor of Dell Publishing's *Candlelight Romances,* briefly contemplated listing the top ten heroines of all times. She quickly discovered that the task was not an easy one, but she did suggest that Hardy's Bathsheba Evardine, Hawthorne's Hester Prynne of *The Scarlet Letter,* and Charlotte Brontë's Jane Eyre—all heroines appearing prior to the twentieth century—would certainly qualify.[1]

The formula for the romance novel calls for a three-dimensional heroine who moves through a kaleidoscope of idealized heroics. Love, hate, ambition, and self-sacrifice build to higher and higher levels of emotional intensity. The reader identifies with these highs and shares in the emotion.

Who hasn't followed the tempestuous theatrics of Scarlett O'Hara in Margaret Mitchell's romance novel, *Gone with the Wind?* What realistic man could have so unequivocally maintained his devotion to family, home, and honor in the face of such taunting beauty as did Ashley Wilkes? The emotional drama of romance fiction has never been exemplified more effectively than when Scarlett O'Hara kneels in a wasted field of radishes before a war-ravaged and dying Tara. As she wretches from hunger and shakes her fist defiantly, her words characterize her strong determination to restore Tara to its pre-war glory.

Written and published at a time when the world was already trembling under the suspenseful political unrest prior to World War II, *Gone with the Wind* cast a magnetic spell upon readers the world over. Hitler was emerging as a German dictator, while his closest ally, Benito Mussolini, was carving a small empire in the weakly defended desert regions of North and East Africa. Readers were easily drawn into the idealized romantic world of gallant men and the heroic Scarlett O'Hara. These characters were acting out roles of another time and place, involved in the trials of war. Sales of the novel at one point were reported to be second only to those of the Bible.

"All great literature is fable in the sense that the meaning or moral is greater than the story itself. It says something about the human condition."[2] As each episode unravels before us, Scarlett O'Hara emerges as a fabulous personality, whose exploits represent the whole woman who takes control of her destiny. Let us consider this novel as the stage upon which Scarlett O'Hara becomes and remains a fable. When she says, "I'll think about it tomorrow," she "represents a lot of people who think the same way."[3]

Consider how the fable theme has become a natural element in the structure of all fiction. Though we may quickly agree that everything in fiction doesn't have to be true, we must make certain that the story "says true things."[4]

Charlotte and Emily Brontë wrote two classic gothic romances that have continued to entertain readers, young and old, since they were first published in the middle of the nineteenth century. Emily's *Wuthering Heights,* centering heavily upon the stormy relationship between Heathcliff and Catherine, unfolds with an intensity that extends to the end of the novel. She tells us the end of her story first, so that we know that three of her novel's principal characters are dead—Catherine, Edgar Linton, and Hindley Earnshaw. This plotting strategy eliminates suspense, the novel's usually main power.[5] Her work becomes realistic, encompassing a feeling of history more so than of fiction. As the novel progresses, the author never loses sight of Heathcliff, the rejected and tormented destroyer of the peace. Catherine's uncontrolled temper becomes an instrument of scorn, which she uses to scorn Edgar and to scold Heathcliff, all for her own selfish ends.[6]

Jane Eyre, published in 1847, became Charlotte Brontë's most popular novel. The plot begins with the childhood of Jane, which gives us a better understanding of Jane as a woman. The story pattern moves in a chronological order, told in first person through the experiences of Jane, who eventually gets the man she loves (not without further pain, however, for he has been blinded in a tragic fire).

Read these two novels. Discover the great differences in how each is told. It is interesting to note that *Jane Eyre* was received with excitement in 1847 when the novel was first published, while Emily's *Wuthering Heights* achieved its greatest success long after publication. Critics tell us that readers today consider Emily's book to be a superior work and that *Jane Eyre* has slipped in esteem. Some of us do not agree, however.[7]

Realism

Novels of the *realism* class come closest to showing life as it is, or was in the past. These characters become entangled in webs of conflict that seem very real. Their struggles gain our sympathy and our concern for their ultimate victories. The writers then lure us along intricate obstacle courses, where we observe our real-to-life figures perform in a manner that also seems genuine to us.

The realist paints a picture of here and now. Escape literature? Yes, for just as we are able to escape into a world far-removed from us in the romance novel, we are also able to forget about our own problems for a time in realist novels. Current controversies, fictionalized historical events with a blend of the romantic, and believable characters who overcome tremendous obstacles, almost always pull us away from our duller moments. Still, realism does not guarantee that all stories will end on a happy note. After all, realism is close to what is real in life, and its purpose must help us to see life as it really is, both happy and sad. Sometimes we even find within it solutions to the problems of the real world, giving us a most satisfying blend of escape and quality fiction.

Steinbeck's *The Grapes of Wrath* is a realistic novel illustrating the plight of the "Okies" who fled Oklahoma during the dust storms of the 1930s. Their story is a harsh revelation that leaves some of us feeling angry that such suffering existed and that so little was done to minimize it. Most of Steinbeck's novels deal with suffering humanity. His characters are determined men and women whose morals, ambitions, social origins, and stamina are thwarted by intolerance, injustice, and greed. Some think that the purpose of Steinbeck's novels is to reveal the sufferings of people and their struggles to overcome their miserable plights. Critics, however, have reexamined *The Grapes of Wrath* and offered us new insights into the author's major purpose. They call the work Steinbeck's "Drama of Consciousness."[8]

Like *The Red Pony*, this story is concluded logically and appropriately within a consistent allegorical message, culminating in "Rosensharn's jesture in the barn. The story of the Joads is completed in the barn. The novel is not about the Joads' quest for security—but about their education."[9] In the beginning of the novel, the family regards itself as an isolated clan. Later they begin to see themselves as a part of the greater human family. The allegorical message is borne within a spiritual movement that ends in changes in family attitude, realized when the family members begin thinking beyond the family.[10]

Steinbeck's earlier novels, *Tortilla Flat* and *Cannery Row,* become allegorical when they present the downtrodden in lives that do not change. The characters do not overcome their problems at the end of the story and are unable to meet the challenges of their time. We picture the people and the events as symbolic of this fate.[11]

Naturalism

Realism becomes *naturalism* when major developments within the story's framework come under the writer's closest scrutiny. The results are bold moves by the writer to expose the tiniest details of behavior, setting, and conflict. Naturalism exposes all that is painful or ugly, no matter how it may affect us.

Though the results of naturalism may be too coarse, even for those less sensitive readers, the stories can still perform a powerful good. Indeed, a societal goal may be the first aim of the writer—to expose evil practices among politicians, manufacturers, individual groups. Such was the chief purpose of Upton Sinclair's *The Jungle,* published in the early part of the twentieth century. Cruel, unjust practices by the meat-packing overlords against poor, uneducated immigrant laborers aroused public indignation and encouraged action.[12]

These passages from the novel shed light upon those practices and upon the sufferings of poor immigrant laborers:

> And so, after little Stanislovas had stood gazing timidly about him for a few minutes, a man approached him, and asked

what he wanted, to which Stanislovas said, "Job." Then the man said "How old?" and Stanislovas answered, "Sixtin." Once or twice every year a state inspector would come wandering through the packing plants, asking a child here and there how old he was; and so the packers were very careful to comply with the law, which cost them as much trouble as was now involved in the boss's taking the document from the little boy, and glancing at it, and then sending it to the office to be filed away. Then he set someone else at a different job, and showed the lad how to place a lard can every time the empty arm of the remorseless machine came to him; and so was decided the place in the universe of little Stanislovas, and his destiny till the end of his days. Hour after hour, day after day, year after year, it was fated that he should stand upon a certain square foot of floor from seven in the morning until noon, and again from half-past twelve till half-past five, making never a motion and thinking never a thought, save for the setting of lard cans. In summer the stench of the warm lard would be nauseating, and in winter the cans would all but freeze to his naked little fingers in the unheated cellar. Half the year it would be dark as night when he went into work, and dark as night again when he came out, and so he would never know what the sun looked like on weekdays. And for this, at the end of the week, he would carry home three dollars to his family, being his pay at the rate of five cents per hour—just about his proper share of the total earnings of the million and three quarters of children who are now engaged in earning their living in the United States. (Upton Sinclair, *The Jungle*, NAL, 1960, pp. 75,76)

Sinclair has introduced the horrors of child labor. He knows what he wants to accomplish, and now he digs deeper into the ugly quagmire, hoping to win new converts to the socialist movement in America:

> There were cattle which had been fed on "whiskey malt," the refuse of the breweries, and had become what the men called "steerly"—which means covered with boils. It was a nasty job killing these, for when you plunged your knife into them they would burst and splash foul smelling stuff into your face; and when a man's sleeves were smeared with blood, and his hands steeped in it, how was he ever to wipe his face, or to clear his eyes so that he could see? It was stuff such as this that made the "embalmed beef" that had killed several times as many United States Soldiers as all the bullets of the Spaniards; only the army beef, besides, was not fresh canned, it was old stuff that had been lying for years in the cellars. (Upton Sinclair, *The Jungle*, NAL, 1960, p. 99)

While Sinclair paints some scenes with the brush of realism, too often the paint is laid down too thickly in colors that turn our stomachs or bring us pain, shock, and anguish. Naturalism occurs, then, when the author deliberately uncovers the ugliest microscopic details in order to achieve a certain reader reaction and to draw support for his causes.

Author Intrusion

The Jungle, written near the beginning of the twentieth century, has a serious defect that should be brought to the student's attention: *author intrusion.* When a writer seizes the reins from the third person narrator and indulges in long discourses of personal opinion, the book loses its creative, imaginative force. In the two excerpts presented previously, the author is quite visible to us. His characters fail to give us their observations and feelings through the third person narrator. Let's revise a portion of these same excerpts and give the story back to the third person storyteller so that we may see how the perspective changes:

Stanislovas stood inside a smelly workshop in an unheated cellar. He had been hungry, but, now, watching a youth filling large cans with warm steaming lard each time the empty arm of the remorseless machine came to him, he felt the nausea rise up from his stomach. He swallowed hard.

In summer, the stench of the warm lard was worse, Papa had told him. But in winter the cans would all but freeze to his fingers.

After a few minutes, he saw an overseer approaching from the far end of the shop. He was a large man who loomed larger as he drew nearer.

The man adjusted his sagging trousers, shuffled his shoulders. "Yeah? Whatcha want, boy?"

"J-Job." He cleared his throat, but he could feel his body trembling.

The man's eyes glared suspiciously. "How old?"

"Sixtin." He knew he did not look that old. He let his eyes shift to the boy attending the lard-dispensing machine. He figured the boy wasn't a year older than he was. He was twelve.

"You sure?" the man asked. "We don't want no trouble with the state inspectors. They come wandering through here all the time."

"Yes, sir." He reached into a pocket for the paper and handed it to the man. He noticed that his hands were not trembling.

The man gave the forged certificate a quick glance. "It's hard work, boy. You come to work before daylight, and it's dark again when you finish the day."

Stanislovas knew what was in store for him. But, at the end of each week, for all the suffering he must endure, he would carry home three dollars to his family, being his pay at the rate of five cents per hour. Then he would not be hungry so often. (An adaptation of selected excerpts from Upton Sinclair's *The Jungle*, Nal, 1960, pp. 75, 76, 99)

Given this approach, we begin to feel the youth's timidity, his loss for words, and his discomfort in the cold, unpleasant surroundings. Through our third person's observations, the horrors of the industry unfold.

4

Six Major Story Elements and Techniques

A *story element* is any part of your story's structure that contributes to its effectiveness. Whether you are analyzing escape fiction or interpretive fiction, you need to determine the author's purpose and the structural techniques that are used to introduce either of several story elements.

Elements are woven together to make organizational patterns, dialogues, theme development, and symbolic references, as well as to facilitate sequential action and reaction within each setting. Elements provide the framework and the flesh of the plot and breathe life into it.

Six Major Story Elements

There are the six key elements you will uncover in most of today's fiction: (1) point-of-view, (2) characterization, (3) atmosphere and tone, (4) conflict, (5) plot, and (6) theme.

Point-of-View

Whose story is it? Who's telling the story? The reader needs this information early in the book. We follow the narrator through the setting as he reports on the actions of any characters and himself. Readers are quick to note errors a first-person narrator might make—reporting on what he could not have seen from where he was positioned or telling us things he could not have known at the time. *Viewpoint* might be considered the position from where the storyteller reports what he sees at the time an incident is taking place.[1]

Point-of-view, a term synonymous with viewpoint, is used more often when discussing the choices an author has for selecting his viewpoint character or storyteller. Will the story be written in the first person, from the major character's point-of-view? or will a minor character be chosen to tell the story? The advantages each choice offers, with explanations and illustrations of these and other methods for presenting point-of-view, are discussed fully in Chapter 6.

Characterization

We can easily describe a character as honest, crooked, deceitful, and so on, but what is more difficult is to use our knowledge of characters to supply essential details supporting our characterizations. There are several methods for characterizing individuals, but three methods are used more often. Suppose your character is brave. (1) Have him perform courageous acts or deeds. (2) Have other characters tell us he's brave. (3) Have the storyteller tell us how brave he is.

The secret of strong *characterization* is in having your characters show us what they are through their motives, actions, and reactions rather than through your narrator. The strongest magic in a stage play, a novel, or a short story occurs regularly from page to page or scene to scene. The writer successfully draws characterizations that become indelible in our memories.[2]

However, let us quickly realize that we do not expect *all* of our characters to become "memorable to the same degree. That's because the same devices you use to make a character memorable ALSO signal to the audience that the character is IMPORTANT."[3]

The Protagonist

Whose story are you writing? That person is usually the main character or the *protagonist,* which may be man, animal, or nature. Your story's purpose is to provide us with a significant segment of this character's behavior over a suitable length of time and space, involving the protagonist with some sort of conflict that leaves him/her changed from the experiences, win, lose, or draw. What does the protagonist need or want? Who or what is preventing him from realizing his goal?

The Antagonist

The *antagonist* is a major character who stands in the way of your protagonist: both are often seeking the same goal. The antagonist does not have to be a person—a tiger, a winter storm, or any other formidable foe will do. Sometimes, the true antagonist is the internal conflict the protagonist experiences.

The Hero or Heroine versus the Villain

Male or female characters around whom a story is structured become *heroes* or *heroines* when they are threatened by some villainous character. When the *villain* sets out to destroy the key male or female figure, tension is built from the fears we hold for the safety of our hero or heroine. Great mental and physical suffering mounts until the final climax and resolution. Contrast this conflict with that of the protagonist who must overcome a personal physical or psychological barrier facing him, or who must defeat some formidable opponent with the same goals.

Stereotypes

Some characters are not important for plotting the main threads of your stories, yet they are important for the setting. Policemen appear in response to a telephone call to prevent a robbery or to catch Pete before he can get away. An elderly, raggedly dressed woman carrying several brown bags she's filled with discards from the street gives us the finer detail of life on a city street. Both are *stereotypes* or typical members of a group, barely noticed and soon to be forgotten. Neither "takes the focus of the audience's attention away from Pete."[4]

Atmosphere

The action, the mood, and the setting provide the sensory images the reader needs for perceiving the who, the what, the how, the where, and the when of any story. As readers, we are on the sidelines of the great visual and emotional panorama unfolding before us, page after page. *Atmosphere* provides both imagery and emotional impact. In many of the stories you analyze, you will find atmosphere is the dominant element for telling the stories.

The following passage is taken from *The Light in the Forest,* Conrad Richter's novel of a four-year-old white child taken and adopted by an Indian, Cuyloga, who had lost his own son. The child lives among them and becomes one of them. When the story opens, the army is moving among the Indian settlements to collect those whites captured by the Indians and return them to their rightful kin. The white child, True Son, now fifteen, is brought to the army encampment and released by his Indian father. He manages to break out, planning to return to his Indian family and friends. But Cuyloga, though it is painful, tracks True Son down and delivers him to the army camped near his village.

> "I gave talking paper that I bring him," he [Cuyloga] told the white guards. "Now he belongs to you."

True Son's spirits are crushed. How could his life among the Indians come to an end? Couldn't they see that he is happier with Cuyloga and his people? He had become one of them. Now he is certain that his life will come to an end. He lies among other captives who are being brought back to the white man's world, and anticipates his death.

Then he becomes certain that his father (Cuyloga) was somewhere close by. He feels the Indian's presence in the scents of red willow bark and dried sumac leaves from his father's pipe. For a moment, the tiniest ray of hope must enter his mind.

Then dusk comes and he hears the voice of the guard, the one they called Del, speak to his father in the Indian tongue.

All Indians are to be out of the camp by nightfall. The ounce of hope True Son might have held is shattered.

He listens intently to the sounds his father makes, deciding that Cuyloga is emptying his pipe and putting it away. Then he feels the Indian's presence and turns to look up at him.

> "Now go like an Indian, True Son," he said in a low, stern voice. "Give me no more shame."

As the plot unravels, the descriptive atmosphere and the thoughts of True Son reveal how deeply entrenched the Indian way of life has become for him. At the same time, we recognize Cuyloga's equally profound sense of pride; we realize this break from the Indian experience is not only painful for True Son but for Cuyloga as well. This scene constructs a wall of conflict that will grow even more insurmountable for the white youth and for his rightful parents.

Conflict

Conflict is generated by obstacles—those imposed by others, by nature, or are self-imposed—that challenge the main character and show us the stuff he/she is made of. From strong characterizations, readers discover the motives that keep the protagonist and antagonist in skillfully woven contests. Given a clearly formed motivation, this conflict of goals mushrooms, spilling over into the lives of other characters and affecting their feelings and actions as well. Once these forces are at work, the plot starts moving and continues to move with actions and counteractions that keep us turning the pages.

Building Contrasts

The life True Son must now face is in sharp *contrast* to his past life, a fact that generates several opportunities for developing close reader identification with all the characters caught up in the tragedy of separation. Solutions should not be readily apparent, and they aren't. Conrad Richter uses every advantage of the Indian experience to draw realistic characterizations of people on either side of the fence. Antagonists emerge on both sides to disrupt the few brief moments of tranquility, and the unrest spreads as the past and the present collide again and again.

When the youth contemplates his life among the whites, we are able to see how little things loom larger in his mind: When he bathes he has to do the woman's work of carrying "with his own hands a bucket of steaming water up the stairs."[5] To make matters even worse for him, his mother insists that he learn to read, whereupon he must spend five afternoons a week in her room with the books. On every seventh morning, his father and his aunt Kate force him to sit between them on one of the benches in the Great Spirit's lodge. He finds it impossible to believe that the God of the whole Universe would dwell in such a walled-in space. He knows better. All Indians know better—the Great Spirit dwells in the open spaces where there are many places for prayer and worship.

External Conflict

When difficulties arise from the setting, anything acting as a deterrent or a wall between your characters and their goals becomes *external conflict*. Examples might include the actions of other characters, as well as storms, floods, or any other opposing situation occurring in nature. Richter's novel introduces bitter conflict with the entrance of the hard-boiled Uncle Wilse, an Indian-hater and an organizer of the township's security. True Son's continuing conflict, however, is in the need to converge two contrasting lifestyles—Indian and white.[6]

Internal Conflict

Values about life often prevent a character from doing harmful things to others or even to himself. Your protagonist may become hard-pressed to behave in ways contrary to his own set of values and begins to suffer *internal conflict*. Here is the opportunity to develop a major crisis for a story or novel by selecting from a reservoir of weaknesses and strengths of character. Bits of information dropped in the earlier parts of the plot—especially information concerning a weakness—can foreshadow what might happen when a character is under pressure. Careful plotting of character traits helps the reader accept the climax, no matter which way it goes—good or bad. If the problem means life or death, the protagonist might rise to meet the occasion in an honorable though often surprising move for survival.

Suppose your protagonist steps out onto the street and discovers a mugging in process. Several young hoodlums are intimidating an old man after relieving him of his wallet and jewelry. Your protagonist glances at the curb and sees that his wife has arrived to pick him up. Their three youngsters are with her. What he does now will let us know what kind of man he is.

Psychological Conflict

Problems do not have to be real; a character may be under great stress because he has not been able to read the true significance of what has happened to him or to someone he cares about. He may be immobilized because of deep-seated fears or phobias and is completely unable to act to forestall a disaster. This *psychological conflict* then creates other conflict that arises from his inaction. In contrast, any action a protagonist might take to remove, reduce, or overcome his psychological conflict may be either internally or externally motivated.

Plot

The step-by-step sequence of events, whether chronological or otherwise, becomes the *plot*. Every incident may introduce several elements of the plot: character, atmosphere, conflict, motivation, symbols, irony, or theme. A series of incidents creates an episode. Short stories are usually written within the bounds of one episode. Novels may have many episodes, some of which may run parallel to each other. The author moves back and forth at intervals, bringing each episode toward a crisis, and connects them at intervals to clarify plot developments and to advance the story line toward the ultimate conclusion. This arrangement of episodes insures unity throughout the novel.

Subplots

The mainstream novel may have *subplots*. Just as episodes connect in novels of one basic plot, keeping the main story line intact, novels having subplots develop each sub-

building a story of broader and deeper coverage. Books with *subplots* often cover several generations, though not always. Their lengths may run over a thousand pages and may be published in two or more volumes; see, for example, *Exodus, War and Remembrance, Shogun,* John Jakes' Civil War giants—*North and South, Love and War,* and a more recent romance, *Heaven and Hell.*

Plotting these novels requires careful planning for each of the separate subplots, allowing them to touch center at the right time. Episodes from either may overlap and keep the subplots purposeful and exciting. Eventually, all points raised are resolved along the way, and the final resolution ties every loose end together.

Foreshadowing

Writers plant little hints or warning signs that foreshadow trouble ahead. Readers might not recognize them for what they are, for the author will not want to reveal too much and destroy the suspense these *foreshadowings* may soon provide. As the suspense develops into some kind of crisis, we recall the information planted earlier and are able to understand the full significance of the plant.

Here are some typical foreshadowing plants:

- A sudden change occurs in a character's behavior.
- Some important papers have been left behind in a sudden departure.
- A set of footprints are discovered in the flower bed outside your bedroom window.

- Unusual odors are emanating from the basement of your home.
- Your housekeeper reports a telephone call from an impatient, unpleasant man.
- A new bride discovers a cryptic note in her husband's coat pocket.

Think how you might use these plant ideas to foreshadow a crisis. The practice will help you establish a better grasp of plotting and will help simplify your analysis of stories.

Suspense

Suspense is generated when readers feel tension and excitement over what has happened and what they sense is about to happen. A new crisis makes us fear for the safety of a character or leaves us feeling uncertain about his success. We become tense; those close to us will sense the excitement in us, too.

Theme

The *theme* is the underlying idea, moral, or lesson about life that is impressed upon the reader. Both the novel and the short story may convey several themes. Some universal themes include the following:

1. Man supports Man
2. Man opposes Man
3. Man supports Himself
4. Man opposes Himself

5. Man supports Nature

6. Man opposes Nature

Specific Themes

Specific themes arise when particular elements produce one or more ideas about man and life that, among many other possibilities, are linked to one or more of the universal themes. When we finish a story, we are left with a strong feeling, a message. We organize what has happened and arrive at a statement about this message or idea.

Some fictional categories don't have a specific theme. The "whodunit" rarely does. The writer takes us along a clue-laden path from the mystery to the moment of resolution; we are hooked into trying to link clues to individual suspects. Before we reach the end, we have probably suspected about everybody, for the author has given all of them strong motives to commit the crime.

Stories lacking themes have one essential reason for being—to entertain us.

Difficult Themes

Some themes are difficult to put into words. These are usually developed by the experimentalist or by authors of other quality fiction. We are left to interpret the theme. We examine the details closely, study the implications, interpret symbols, and pay strict attention to characterization from the descriptive atmosphere. You will see how such themes are developed when you study the chapters on story elements, and you will get additional coverage in the chapters on short story and novel patterns.

Here are some popular themes:

- Perseverance can make you a winner.
- Lies are told to protect the ones we love; too often we live to regret them.
- Gold may be deceiving; we may find we've given up something more precious in exchange.

Dominant Elements

Some story patterns require one or more *dominant element.* The author decides which of the six elements will achieve the desired effect. Remember, quality stories often use character and setting or some other combination to produce a particular result. Keep this in mind when you are analyzing the story elements.[7]

Read the following stories and note the dominant elements used in them:

Short Story	Dominant Elements
"The Sniper," by Liam O'Flaherty	conflict, irony
"The Secret Life of Walter Mitty," by James Thurber	character, fantasy
"By the Waters of Babylon," by Stephen Vincent Benét	atmosphere
"The Piece of String" by Guy de Maupassant	theme

Plotting Techniques

A *plotting technique* is how the writer achieves a specific result: his/her method of patterning stories, of producing symbols for several distinct purposes, of creating imagery, of using flashbacks to provide information the reader needs, of producing effects such as humor or irony, and a number of other special techniques the professional may choose to heighten the reader's interest. A writer's technique in plotting and shaping the story is the result of his/her knowledge, experience and personal choices.

5

Eight Supportive Elements and Techniques

You have learned six major elements that help writers shape their story patterns that help move the plot and provide reader satisfaction. Sometimes, however, writers need additional tools to shape stories, especially in building a successful novel. These tools will provide writers with:

1. a technique for introducing material from the past to bolster or to explain an action in the present, or to provide information that makes a future situation credible;

2. a way to accent any particular element within the plot;

3. a technique for plotting the unexpected;

4. a method for presenting a one-sided argument to draw loyalty and support for a cause;

5. techniques for introducing social, economic, or politi-

cal problems in a critical or ridiculous light to encourage support and action from readers;

6. techniques that place story elements in an unreal frame of time, place and, situation;

7. elements for telling a story to teach a lesson; and

8. a technique for weaving spiritual and/or symbolic references into the plot to present a moral.

These eight *supportive elements* or *techniques,* each requiring study, practice, and application are known, respectively, as (1) flashbacks; (2) symbols; (3) irony; (4) propaganda; (5) satire; (6) fantasy; (7) parables; and (8) allegory. You will want to be able to analyze the purposes and the effectiveness of each as you uncover them in your study selections.

Flashbacks

A *flashback* stops the forward thrust of a story in order to take the reader back in time. Perhaps a writer needs to prepare the reader before a characterization can be accepted. For example, the reader may need to know that the character has some particular skill with locks before he can believe the action the character is about to take to free himself from a predicament. Of course, the writer could go back into the story and add a couple of scenes, characterizing his protagonist in a manner compatible with the feats he must perform at a later point. At times, however, a brief flashback accents some characteristic and may be all that is needed to validate the action. The danger here is in making the switch in time too close to the beginning of the story.

The choice of timing is critical. If the protagonist is to stand as a whole-life character, he must present a whole-life image in the beginning. Descriptions of an implied past, his behavior in the immediate surroundings, dialogues, and his thoughts should be enough to give us vivid impressions of his connections with the setting and with other characters.

If the writer stopped the action for a flashback *only* to supply information rather than to provide additional information, the reader is left searching for some type of anchor from the present with which to associate the new information given in the flashback. If he doesn't find one, the protagonist, who hasn't yet been made important in the present, becomes a vague, stereotyped image.[1]

Readers frown upon flashbacks that appear close to the beginning of your story. If your story seems to need one at the beginning, perhaps you should come up with another opener. If the information is so important that it can't be covered in the present—through dialogues and thought—then you will probably fare better by beginning your story with the time, place, and events of your flashback.[2]

When you are approaching a formidable crisis in at least the middle of your story, a flashback can increase the excitement and the importance of the obstacle as well as provide a subtle bit of information that will become the key to its resolution. What is important, then, is the timing and significance of the flashback. The flashback should be brief, and it should occur only after the story is anchored in the present.[3]

Symbols

Symbols can be most effective for performing a number of specific story effects. A rose, a bird, an ocean's tide, a snake, and a bleeding heart are symbols used by many writers. Symbols help unify the plot of a novel or story, as in Hawthorne's *The Scarlet Letter,* or accent the theme, as in his "Dr. Heidegger's Experiment." Symbols are introduced to serve a variety of purposes, from foreshadowing evil or good, or sharpening the effect of parallel story elements.[4]

Irony

One or more types of *irony* can appear in either genre of fiction. Actually, our own lives are often gladdened or saddened by the ironies we encounter almost daily, usually without giving them special notice.

Situation Irony

O. Henry used *situation irony* quite effectively in his humorous short stories. Most of you will recall his "The Ransom of Red Chief" from your school reading experiences. When two kidnappers try to collect a ransom for the boy they are holding in the hills outside of town, they fail to account for the agonies the youngster's pranks unleash upon them. A series of efforts to collect the ransom from the youth's guardian, intermingled with the difficulties the kidnappers face in managing and containing the boy, lead to their change of heart, completing the pattern for situation irony.

Dramatic Irony

In this situation the speaker is obviously making statements to get his listeners to believe one thing, while you as an observer know he means the opposite of what he's telling them.

Consider the speech of Mark Antony following the brutal stabbing of Julius Caesar: Mark Antony knows the people have turned against Caesar. Through the power of dramatic irony, he gets them to listen and to change their attitudes about Caesar. As readers or viewers of the events on the stage, we see the changes taking place and note the crowds begin to surge forward toward Caesar's murderers. We know what Mark Antony set out to do, and we follow his success. The use of this technique is called *dramatic irony.*

Verbal Irony

Verbal irony is also a regular experience for us; it occurs whenever we make a statement that is the exact opposite of what we feel or think. For instance, when somebody has done something or has said something that angers or annoys you, your response might be: "Well, I like that!" "You're too kind!" "Aren't you the smart one?" "Well, thank you!"

Propaganda

Propaganda is getting people to believe what you want them to believe without telling them directly why you want them to believe it. Propaganda doesn't have to be based upon lies, or even half-truths; every fact laid before us may be absolutely true. What makes the book a propaganda device happens when the writer has ignored the scales of truth. He has not balanced the scales; he has not used equal proportions of the two elements of truth—its advantages and disadvantages. The propagandist exploits only the advantages or the disadvantages of a truth, and he intentionally withholds his purposes for presenting only one side of any issue.

The naturalism of Upton Sinclair's *The Jungle* was intended to draw ire out of its readers and to increase the ranks of the socialist party in America. Sinclair does not tell us this. He presents an ugly picture of inhuman practices within Chicago's meat-packing industry. At the expense of using stereotyped characters, the writer is seen and heard regularly as he uses propaganda to deliver his message.

Satire

With *satire* we discover that writing may have sharp teeth. Just as the propagandist paints a one-sided view of truth, the satirist paints unflattering caricatures of groups or individuals to embarass them or to enlighten the public in the hope of instigating reactions that will lead to change. Sometimes the target is a group or individual whose performances are questionable, unproductive, dangerous, or simply unfashionable.

Jonathan Swift's *Gulliver's Travels* has become a classic example of this category. The English government and the customs of eighteenth-century English society are made to appear obstinate, whimsical, narrow-minded, or incompetent. Educational practices are, at best, crude and impractical. Laws are not based upon judicious consideration but upon the whim or silly quackery of governing individuals and administrators.

Fantasy

Swift's *Travels* takes us into the realms of *fantasy,* a colorful vehicle for presenting his satire in thought-provoking, acid-wielding reports and observations. Stories based upon unreal characters in unreal situations who move about in fairy-tale settings are the frame and pattern for fantasy.

An example of this writing strategy is found in George Orwell's *Animal Farm.* Orwell uses the plot and the animal characters to symbolize the Russian Revolution and the party struggles that led to internal division and slaughter.[5]

Orwell was a socialist in England before war broke out in Europe in 1939. In that year Joseph Stalin turned his back against the allies and signed the infamous Russo-German Nonaggression Pact. Orwell became disenchanted with the Russians. *Animal Farm* might be seen as his protest against that country's betrayal of England and her growing socialist movement.[6]

Parables

Jesus Christ taught through *parables,* or stories with a lesson or moral. John Steinbeck used parables in his thematic structuring of *The Pearl,* his short novel that some critics call a novella, and others call a symphony of symbolic musical themes, such as "Song of the Family," "Song of Evil," and "Song of the Enemy." These and other "songs" are symbolic of good or evil as they occur in the plot.[7]

Here we have the unfolding of a tragic tale, one that is dressed in symbols: night and day, goodness and evil. The parable develops as each of the transitional "songs" define the meaning of the pearl. These carry us along a trail marked with tragedy, until we see the pearl returned to the sea. The parable, or moral, is now complete: man's spiritual struggles against material wealth is a sojourn against social and economic barriers that eventually bring failure and personal tragedy.[8]

Allegory

The ending of *The Pearl* completes an allegorical theme that speaks of futility. Kino and Juana lose something more than the wealth denied to them—they lose their infant son, Coyotito. *Allegories* such as these explore truths or generalizations about the nature of man, using symbolic, spiritual, or figurative clues. They can contain hidden spiritual meanings that reach beyond the literal sense of the text.

Part Two
Analyses of Fiction Elements and Techniques

6

Choosing a Point-of-View

Whose story are you telling? Who will tell it best? Sometimes you will want your principal character to tell the story. At other times, you will assign this duty to a subordinate character. Although the importance of this choice may seem minor, it can make a big difference. For instance, in stories where your principal character's exploits involve flattery of some kind, you will fare better having a subordinate character report on them; otherwise, you risk having your principal character appear vain or conceited.[1]

You must keep in mind that your storyteller has to have the best opportunities for on-the-scene observations of the principal character. A good choice would be a narrator who will be able to get good second-hand observations from relatives, close friends, and household servants. He will then have substantial knowledge of the principal character's behavior, his petty gripes, his private choices of reading fare, and his selection of friends and entertainment. Such information provides your readers with *three-dimensional characters.*[2]

Physical Point-of-View

Where is your narrator positioned as he views and reports what he perceives through his five senses? Your narrator must be placed where he can perceive any action, mood, or part of the setting you want conveyed to your readers. This positioning provides us with a *physical point-of-view.* For example, if you are standing at the end of a crowded street when an explosion occurs in a building two blocks away, you will not be able to see and sense as much as would someone inside the building.[3]

Errors in Viewpoint

Normally the problem is not in getting the storyteller close to the situation but is in having him report something that he could not have seen from his viewing point, or *viewpoint.* Read the following passage. Can you spot the errors in viewpoint?

> The door opened wide. Mrs. Adams was a big woman who always smiled when she saw me pass her house on my way to or from school.
>
> "Selling magazines again, Joey?" Her smile made her big brown eyes sparkle.
>
> "I'm delivering telegrams for Mr. Gerryman," I said.
>
> "Oh?" She pressed the flat of her palms against her sides and straightened her back.

> She took the envelope and opened it. Then she stood there in her sea-blue print with the tiny, navy-blue anchors. She wore a little white apron, tied with a wide, full bow in back.
>
> The smile left her face. "Oh, dear," she cried.

What was included in this first person report that the storyteller could not have seen? Was there something he could not have known? Obviously, Joey could not have seen Mrs. Adams's bow tied in the back. The woman would have had to turn her back to him, or perhaps the writer could have added a mirror behind her. Now what about that smile? Could Joey have known each time Mrs. Adams had seen him pass her house? No. Therefore, he could not have seen that she "always smiled when she saw me pass her house." He could have reported, "Mrs. Adams always smiled when I waved to her on my way to or from school."

Errors like these often turn up in your manuscripts, but most of them will not get past the close scrutiny of writers who edit and revise carefully. The professional experience of the editor assigned to work with you on the manuscript can also help free it of such errors.

Choosing a Point-of-View

Novels by beginning or unfamiliar writers are usually written in first person. First person accounts have a natural flow of thoughts and action and hold a presence, which has a familiar ring. We are able to identify with the storyteller, for it is as if the narrator is right beside us, giving us these firsthand reports. First person novels also allow us to experience realistically each event that unfolds on the printed pages. The effect is like having the writer, through his narrator, take us by the arm and tell us everything that is happening.[4]

Of course, some novels would have failed if they had been written in first person. To use the first person point-of-view your novel must be told entirely by a single viewpoint character. The writer has to identify strongly with this narrator; any driving motivations must grow out of the genuine, personal ambitions, confrontations, or beliefs, and his actions must agree with the character you have allowed him to become. A first person narration can be troublesome if your fictional character is larger than life—an idol of the silver screen, the president of the United States, or some notorious gangster—for then a third person viewpoint will provide varied impressions of your principal characters, giving a more detailed examination of their true natures.[5]

There are at least five POV (point-of-view) choices:

1. *First person narrator:* Your *major character* tells us his/her story.

2. *First person narrator:* A *minor character* tells the story. He must have certain advantages that make him the best choice for telling another character's story.

3. *Third person, objective POV:* Each character lets the reader perceive all dialogue and actions. The reader can grasp implications in the tone of the speaker's spoken words and in his actions, but the objective POV never allows the narrator to enter the mind of a character to tell us what that character is thinking.

4. *Third person, limited omniscient POV:* Our third person narrator is allowed to enter the mind and give us the

thoughts of only one character, the one whose story is being told.

5. *Third person, omniscient POV:* We can know the thoughts of any number of characters; the third person narrator, always on the sidelines, sees and knows all.

Samples of POV Choices

First Person—Major Character POV

> A large figure appeared for a split second at the lighted entrance of the great house. He lurched forward sharply and disappeared into the shadows on my right. There sat the rose garden, covered in a black shroud cast by two great water oaks.
>
> I shrank back into the brush bordering the horseshoe drive, sank to my knees to stop them from shaking. I was afraid for Chancey. The intruder could have seen me come out of the cellar earlier. Could he also know that Chancey was still down there, taking pictures of what we had uncovered?
>
> The hinges on the cellar door squeaked. I swallowed hard, catching my breath. Chancey had to be warned of the new danger.
>
> My friend's own warning came back to me. "Skeet," he had said, "you worry too much." I don't. Just enough, I think.
>
> Chancey . . . now I knew why that name stuck to him. . . .

Skeet is our first-person POV character. This is his story, and he is the storyteller. Skeet can tell us about himself and his father:

> Sometimes I get feelings of a disaster heading in my direction long before I see the first signs of trouble stirring. I got that feeling at suppertime when my dad jumped up from the table to answer the telephone.

He scribbled something on a pad, tore out the sheet, and he was gone, like one of those striped lizards that shoot across your path in the woods and scare the living daylights out of you.

I dusted the pad with shavings from a pencil sharpener, brushed the page gently, and shook the shavings into a wastebasket. My heart skipped two beats. The address was that of Chancey's parents. My dad would go there and learn that Chancey and I had left his house together. That'd be the end of the secret Chancey and I shared. If Chancey hadn't returned home, he was in serious trouble.

I would have told my dad about the stuffed owl. But Chancey would have felt betrayed.

About an hour later, I heard Dad's patrol car enter the carport. In seconds, he was inside, standing there looking at me with those x-ray eyes that have a way of getting inside your mind. "Where's Chancey? Out with it, Skeet!"

First Person Narrator—Minor Character POV

An author might choose a minor character to serve as the storyteller. The activities of that popular sleuth from Scotland Yard, Sherlock Holmes, usually keeps everyone guessing. When Dr. Watson, a minor character, asks questions, the reader gets the answers, but only when Detective Holmes is ready to let everyone in on them.[6]

The Great Gatsby, a novel by F. Scott Fitzgerald, uses Nick Carraway to tell Gatsby's story. Nick becomes Gatsby's neighbor. Here he is able to observe who goes in and out of his neighbor's place. What he is not able to get from these people, he gets from the butler and the chauffeur at various times.[7]

The glitter, the alcohol, the myths, and the final tragedies surrounding Gatsby come to life through a succession of parties, from conversations with those closest to Gatsby, and from others who regularly manage to crash his parties. Nick is able to give us his impressions of all that he sees, hears, and learns from others who are close to the man.[8]

Third Person—Objective POV

The third person, objective POV is used most often in fictional drama. We are not taken inside the minds of any character. Whatever we are able to learn comes from the thoughts and feelings as expressed through dialogues and action on the stage. Some authors have used this POV successfully. Still, it is a difficult POV to maintain since it is so easy inadvertently to break the rules of objectivity.[9]

Study the following passage (Josh and Brick are taking a break after stringing their lines across the lake for catfishing):

> From Scout's Landing, harsh sounds of a motor being pushed to the limit, drowned the late evening orchestra of mosquitoes whining in Josh's face and ears. Josh stiffened.
>
> Brick slapped at a mosquito caught in the light of their small lantern, pushed his chair back from the picnic table. He stood and faced the lake.
>
> Bright twin beams bounced across the dark waters of Lake Warren. Brick threw his cards on the table. "Somebody's truck's stuck in the sand."
>
> A pistol shot cracked across the water. A voice cried out. A door slammed.
>
> Brick sprang over the picnic table and raced for their canoe. "C'mon, Josh!"
>
> He pushed the canoe from its dry dock in the grasses, and stood there at the water's edge, holding the chain.
>
> Josh smothered the lantern.
>
> "Bring the lantern with you!" Brick called.

Brick steadied the boat while Josh boarded her.

The chain clinked and rattled as he tossed it over onto the floor of the boat. They dug the paddles into the shallow water and moved out into deeper water.

"It's crazy," Josh said.

"No, it ain't."

"We could get shot!"

"No, we won't. There's a small inlet to the left of the landing. We'll go in there. I've fished from that spot. There's a footpath along the banks. Leads to the boathouse."

"What's that?" Josh whispered, but the voice was magnified on the water.

"A boat motor."

"It is!" Josh exclaimed.

"Paddle! He won't see us."

Their small craft moved easily over the quiet waters as both paddles dug deeply into its depths. Soon they slowed and maneuvered the vessel into a small clearing just visible in the moonlight.

Obviously, a third person is telling the story; the descriptions of the harsh sounds in the night, and the reporting of the action and the words spoken by our two characters, Josh and Brick, come from a third person narrator. The narrator reports on what any sideline individual could perceive—sensory responses to events passing before him. Note that the story is being told objectively. We only learn what the characters think and feel through their dialogue. Through the characters' speech readers are able to perceive other details as well: disappointment, fear, suspicion, bravery and other implications. The story will remain in the objective viewpoint unless the author tells the reader what either Josh or Brick is thinking.

Third Person—Limited Omniscient POV

You may elect to tell your story in third person, limited omniscient POV. Everything the reader learns, sees, hears, and feels is provided by a third person who can also see through the mind, eyes, ears, and emotions of one character. Again, the POV character may be a major or a minor one.

From Guy de Maupassant, a French short story writer born in the middle of the nineteenth century, came some of the best short stories ever plotted by any writer. This author has been recognized throughout the world for his use of theme as a dominant element. Some critics have called him "the Father of the modern short story."[10]

"The Necklace" has become a classic. This story is of a woman whose false pride brings her years of toil and suffering. Upon that all elements of the plot are nurtured.

Theme is again dominant in "The Piece of String." This time, the story hinges upon a single, innocent act of Maitre Hauchecome of Breaute, who arrived in Goderville on market day. Farmers and their families from the surrounding farm communities were descending in great numbers to present the products of their labors.

> . . . he [Maitre Hauchecome] was directing his steps toward the public square, when he perceived upon the ground a little piece of string. Maitre Hauchecome, economical like a true Norman, thought that everything useful ought to be picked up, and he bent painfully, for he suffered from rheumatism. He took the bit of thin cord from the ground and began to roll it carefully when he noticed Maitre Malandain, the harnessmaker, on the threshold of his door, looking at him. They had heretofore had business together on the subject of a halter, and they

were on bad terms, being both good haters. Maitre Hauchecome was seized with a sort of shame to be seen thus by his enemy, picking a bit of string out of the dirt. He concealed his "find" quickly under his blouse, then in his trousers' pocket; then he pretended to be still looking on the ground for something which he did not find, and he went toward the market, his head forward, bent double by his pains.

("The Piece of String," by Guy de Maupassant)

The third person narrator has entered the mind of our protagonist, Maitre Hauchecome, whose perceptions of others in the market town will be shared with us. The storyteller does not enter the minds of other characters. Their thoughts are handled objectively unless perceived through the senses of Maitre Hauchecome, whose tragic story is being told.

Third Person—Omniscient POV

If the author chooses a third person, omniscient POV, the narrator can go inside the minds of every significant character. In Douglas Reeman's war-at-sea adventure, *To Risks Unknown,* the third person can see the perceptions and thoughts of several characters: the admiral, the captain, and several crew members aboard the corvette, *Thistle*. Each of these individuals takes his turn carrying the POV responsibilities.

Two POV characters emerge in Lynn Hall's young adult novel, *Gently Touch the Milkweed.* Janet, aged seventeen, suddenly realizes she is a woman when she becomes infatuated with Mel, an older married man who is the editor of the town's newspaper. Each gives us perceptions and thoughts about the other as well as perceptions about other characters and events.

Breaking the Rules

Are POV guidelines ever broken? Yes, they are. Damon Knight, novelist, short story writer and editor, has broken the rules of POV and surprised and shocked his readers by violating expectations.[11] For example, one long-accepted rule of viewpoint states: "Don't use first person in writing about a character who is going to die."[12] Knight explains, "I once broke the rule in a crime story, told in first person by a criminal working a scam on a police detective. Because of the first person narrative, my reader was confident that the criminal would survive; but he didn't. The last line was, 'See what I mean, Satan?' "[13]

Writers who break the rules of POV must still make their innovations work, and beginners may want to learn how to make the rules work for them before they search for ways to break them.

Single Versus Multiple Viewpoint

Let's simplify the ideas presented here. First, we may choose one or more characters to tell the story. If we use only one character to tell the story from beginning to end, we have used a *single viewpoint character*. If the plot becomes complex, including subplots or important events where one viewpoint character cannot be present, you might need to select another character whose thoughts and actions we can follow throughout the event. In such a case, the story will be reported by a third person in an omniscient point-of-view. These additional storytellers are able to see and report things that give our stories the breadth and depth not possible in single viewpoint stories.[14]

Although it is probably easiest for the beginning novelist to tell all through the eyes of a single, lead character in a first person account, this single viewpoint limits opportunities for expanding the frame of the story. The story one wants to tell will determine whether one or more storytellers are needed.[15]

The *multiple viewpoint* keeps you from being stuck with one character for the duration of your book. When you close a scene you can skip to another storyteller who takes over.[16]

Examining the works of several writers sharpens our perceptions of how viewpoint may be handled effectively in different ways. This analysis affects our sense of what works and what doesn't. It also teaches us more about developing viewpoint characters than what we can learn by reading volumes of materials on the subject.[17]

It's Your Turn

Show and tell are only two parts of the learning process. For most of us, the most important part of learning is to apply what we have learned. Examine the three excerpts that follow. Decide which POV was used. Whose story is it? Who's telling it?

A

> His Majesty desired I would take some other opportunity of bringing all the rest of his enemy's ships into his ports. And so unmeasurable is the ambition of princes, that he seemed to think of nothing less than reducing the whole empire of Blefescu into a province, and governing it by a Viceroy; of destroying the Big-Endian exiles, and compelling that people to break the smaller end of their eggs, by which he would remain the sole monarch of the whole world.
>
> (Jonathan Swift, *Gulliver's Travels*)

B

Oftener and oftener, as time went on, did his glance settle on the girl (Blanche) herself. Her face was bowed forward and covered with her hands, and she was shaken at intervals by the convulsive hiccup of grief. Even thus she was not an unpleasant object to dwell upon, so plump and yet so fine, with a warm brown skin, and the most beautiful hair, Denis thought, in the whole world of womankind. Her hands were like her uncle's, but they were in place at the end of her young arms, and looked infinitely soft and caressing. He remembered how her blue eyes had shown upon him, full of anger, pity, and innocence. And the more he dwelt on her perfections, the uglier death looked, and the more deeply was he smitten with penitence at her continued tears. Now he felt that no man could have the courage to leave a world which contained so beautiful a creature; and now he would have given forty minutes of his last hour to have unsaid his cruel speech.

(Robert Louis Stevenson, "The Sire de Malétroit's Door")

C

September was the last of the tourist season. One lone, middle-aged gentleman, casually dressed, approached the rail and looked out toward a lighted buoy bobbing about in the sea.

A minute later, a dark-haired woman, perhaps thirty or younger, her hair combed back tightly and woven in a single braid, stood at the entrance to the lounge. Her eyes darted about the empty tables, where lighted candles cast shimmering shadows about the floor.

She must have seen him then. She went over to the rail and stood there beside him, looking out toward the receding tide.

"Bon voyage," she said, without looking at him.

"Fascinating," he said.

"I could have pretended I didn't know," she said. "It's better this way."

"September's already upon us," he said. "Perhaps you should have worn a wrap."

"Your book . . . it's finished now. I'm glad you let me read it. Amazing how much you can learn about a writer . . . from reading his books, I mean."

He said nothing. Just stood there, leaning against the iron rail, his eyes staring straight ahead. She turned and looked at him for a long time, her lips growing tremulous. Then, "Bon voyage," she repeated.

"Sharks out there," he said.

He didn't get a response from her. He waited a few seconds before turning his eyes to the empty space where she had stood. Then he looked back just in time to catch a brief glimpse of her before she disappeared inside the lounge.

He took a deep breath and exhaled with apparent ease. A smile crept into the corners of his mouth. . . .

Let's see how well you did.

A. Excerpt from *Gulliver's Travels:* first person—major character POV. This is Gulliver's story, and he is the storyteller.

B. Excerpt from "The Sire de Malétroit's Door": third person—limited omniscient POV. Denis's story is being told by an unseen third person who can tell us what one character, Denis, perceives.

C. Third person—objective POV. The third person narrator only tells what can be perceived by the senses. All thoughts, feelings, characterizations, and conflict are revealed to us through the words and actions of the characters.

This is the story of a writer and of a woman whose affair is coming to an abrupt end.

The Right Viewpoint

"The amateur is apt to cling stubbornly to the story, just as he wrote it; the professional will not permit himself the luxury of such an attitude."[18] Experienced writers change what is necessary to get the best story. They may have to start at the beginning and do it all over again. In the end, a more exciting story may be produced that had been concealed behind the wrong point-of-view.[19]

Time has brought changes in what is and what is not acceptable in selecting your viewpoint. Novels have been using multiple viewpoints for years, but until a few years ago, short stories were developed under stiffer rules. In this genre point-of-view technique has drastically changed. In many short stories, you will discover shifts in viewpoint. Still, the author is given this freedom only when there is no other way to tell the story.[20]

Read several short stories and analyze the author's viewpoint. Does the viewpoint shift back and forth? Does the shift confuse you? If not, what did the author do to accomplish the smooth transition between shifting viewpoints? Would a single viewpoint have worked better?

These questions will arise often as you analyze short stories and novels and when you pattern your own stories. Beginners will first want to develop skills in handling a single viewpoint in shorter fiction, for many obstacles are there for you to overcome. When you've worked with a variety of viewpoints and feel confident that you can manage a smooth transition, go ahead and try your hand at shifting viewpoints.

7

A Hierarchy of Story People

Characters from some stories stick with us all of our lives. Others are forgotten almost as soon as we have finished the stories. What makes a character or a story memorable?

"Today's realistic fiction owes a lot to the romantic tradition."[1] The romantic tradition was given birth in those earlier tales of Charlemagne, King Arthur, and Sir Francis Drake. The refererence here is not to the commercial romance category, but to the heroic proportions of those characters and others, such as Richard of the Lionheart, who led great armies in a costly crusade to recover the Holy Land from the Moslems. Pain, jeopardy, and heroic deeds made these characters memorable and sympathetic.[2]

There are certain characters that almost everyone remembers. We have followed their lives and shared their victories and defeats, their hopes and their pain. Scarlett O'Hara, David Copperfield, Rhett Butler, Tiny Tim, Huckleberry Finn, Jane Eyre, Heathcliff, and Hester Prynne are only a few who have become memorable to millions of readers throughout the world.

Character Identification

You and I want to read about people with whom we can identify easily; for, when we care about them, their stories become more readable. We have to feel an intense involvement with the story's major characters. Our caring helps us to know enough about them to understand their motives, good or bad. We examine our own motives, using ourselves as models when we analyze character. Remember the subtle cuts and innuendoes you made when you recoiled from unpleasantness and struck back for revenge? Can you also remember the warmth, the love, and the gratitude you felt when others responded to your needs with kindness and sympathy? Mean people nurture mean reactions. We study ourselves by asking questions often and coming up with honest answers. We also look objectively at and within ourselves while studying other people with warmth and concern. Our minds and our hearts are opened to human nature performing at its best or worst. Each of us is different. As an aspiring writer or as a student you will be able to recognize, understand, or create more people who are "quite new."[3]

The student reaches one of his highest goals when he is able to recognize and define those qualities of fiction that produce the magic that "moves us to tears."[4] Writers who can make us experience such sentiments about what happens to ordinary people are both talented and sensitive; however, when their efforts are poorly developed or when the technique is attempted too often, the writer is branded as a mushy sentimentalist. When a writer attempts to stir our emotions and move us to tears, and he fails, the novel weakens; in the short story, any unneccessary sentiments will lead to rejection.[5]

Convincing Characters

How do writers make their characters convincing? Writers must know more about their story people than they ever tell us. They invent a whole person—one who has special interests and skills and a past that will conjure a variety of twist and turns in the plot. They establish weaknesses as well, for the whole character must also be very human. Finally, they have their characters behave in a manner that is both convincing and inevitable.[6]

These characters have something "quite new" about them, raising them a notch above characters from people a writer meets on the street or at work. Characters drawn from real life do not always work in fiction; the writer does not know enough about them to impose upon them his ideas of what they are and how they should act or react. Imaginary characters are given a "whole life"—more than enough personality to make them appear convincing for the student who will probe even deeper than most readers.[7]

This does not mean that characters will not be drawn from a writer's experiences with people. Where else can one get ideas about people, their conflicts, and their influences upon others? Instead, once you start building your characters for the roles they will play, draw upon a storehouse of many characteristics, appearances, events, solutions, and the emotional effects needed to invent characters with whole, "new" identities.

You may recognize fiction characters as people you have known, even though you won't know everything about these characters, just as you couldn't possibly know everything about an individual who lives in a house or an apartment next to you. *Identification* of certain qualities these individuals have makes you care about them. You care because the author has given them a "real-to-life" but credible character based upon compatible information on the emotional, psychological, and behavioral traits of many individuals.

This new individual is a composite structuring that requires much consideration. The story analyst should be quick to note "out-of-character" descriptions that do not fit a character's actions or appearances. How many times have you recognized this flaw in television productions? How many times have you switched stations because you grew disgusted with the phony character reactions in a critical situation? He would not have deserted his family, you protest. In other words, the writer has failed to give us a character who would desert his family. The character's actions are not credible. In short, earlier information about the character should have revealed a tendency toward irresponsibility. When this trait is not made clear to us, we cannot believe he'd do such a thing—under pressure or not. We don't have to like the character. We must find his actions credible.

Two Classifications of Characters

The two classes of fictional characters are (1) kinetic and (2) static.

Kinetic Characters

If your characters show growth and change as your plot develops, they are *kinetic characters*. The principal characters of most novels are of this type. The novel is long and broad enough to allow several different stages. There is room to provide much more of a person's inner self, his past as well as the current self, completing a whole person with human or inhuman qualities. Whatever successes these people achieve is attributable to their personal growth and to their willingness to change.[8]

Static Characters

Some principal characters are *static characters*. They do not change considerably, and we don't mind because we want them to be what they are. We are practically hypnotized by their larger-than-life qualities displayed in idealized settings.[9]

Scarlett O'Hara and Rhett Butler remain basically unchanged throughout the many crises each faces. Rhett Butler is a blockade runner who is wiser at the end, but he remains the gallant, heroic figure throughout. Scarlett remains the industrious, scheming woman who, faced with a real crisis at the very end of the novel, leaves us assured that her audacious inner spirit will again help her overcome its challenges.

How Many Characters Are Needed?

Story people serve a variety of roles, each essential for the completion of some story function. Some characters are introduced briefly and never mentioned again. The *hierarchy of story characters* includes the major characters, a few prominent subordinate characters, and any number of characters considered to be extras.

Major Characters

Major characters are often referred to as the principal characters. These become the protagonists and antagonists, the heroes or heroines, and the villains. What they mean to you is determined by how skillfully they're crafted and on how well you interpret their characterizations and the roles they play.

Minor Characters

Minor characters are also known as subordinate characters. These fit into the broad middle position of the character hierarchy. Some of these may be given significant roles, especially in the novel. They are essential for the development of episodes and subplots, offering important opportunities for contrasts. You may even find that subordinate characters often tell the protagonists' stories.

Subordinates As Extras

Subordinate characters at the bottom of the character hierarchy operate the elevators, the buses, the telephone switchboards, the taxis, the department stores, and the other businesses and professional services we encounter in our own lives. They are the extras at parties, in the supermarkets, at fires, on buses, on ships, in storms, and at work or play everywhere. Each serves to lend reality and color to settings and situations.

The Foil

A technique for providing especially sharp characterizations is to use a foil. The *foil* is a subordinate character whose presence and contributions to a conversation or to the setting brings out the worst or the best in the protagonist. The foil is usually in sharp contrast to the protagonist. Arthur Conan Doyle gave us Dr. Watson, who was always ready to ask the questions we wanted answered. What did Sherlock Holmes's latest discovery mean? What connections should we make of Detective Holmes's goings and comings? Dr. Watson is just as confused as we are. He is a stand-in for the confused reader—a sharp contrast to the expert detective Holmes.

Local Color

Local color gives the reader the uniqueness and essential qualities that lend a touch of realism and romance to a specific setting. San Francisco becomes more real to us when we imagine the cable cars grating along the rails, when we read of Knob Hill and recall the fashionable homes of the new rich at the close of the nineteenth century, when we envision the waterfront and the boats docked along the fishermen's wharves, when we imagine the sunrise over the red tiled roofs that dip and rise with the irregular elevations of the earth, when we are reminded of the Golden Gate Bridge and the waters of San Francisco Bay, when we follow the characters into Chinatown and its colorful variety of shops with their tourists.

Puppet Characters

Some writers find themselves struggling with plot, using *cardboard characters* like puppets being pulled along by the action. Characterizations are shaped to fit the events only after the events are framed in some preset pattern. As story analysts, you rarely find these *puppet characters* in the published short story. In the novel, instances of puppet characterizations are not as rare. The characters are frail figures with little real character, and we cannot fully identify with them.[10]

These characters have not been allowed to become themselves. They are drawn onto the plains in a long line of covered wagons. Suddenly, the horizon on two or more sides is lined with hostile Indians. Just as we are made to fear for their lives, the U.S. cavalry races onto the field with bugles blaring. The reader feels disappointed, for the characters have not been given the opportunity to solve their problem. They are lifeless, flat puppets of a plot that does not generate character.[11]

The solution might have been for the writer to determine where he could have planted the seeds to foreshadow the arrival of the cavalry. Did Lt. Cary hear the fort commander mention the arrival of a new detachment of volunteers? Was Lt. Cary allowed to become a dependable character in earlier actions? Does he have the qualities that make the reader fear for his safety and pull for him because he has the mixed qualities that make him human? Don't hurry to get a crisis resolved. If the cavalry must arrive, let the moment come after Lt. Cary has succeeded in using his knowledge and daring to turn the tide of conflict.[12]

While it is important for us to plant seeds to characterize individuals with qualities that make later feats credible, simply planting these seeds alone anywhere in the story is not enough. A writer must also know *when* to plant these seeds. Writers who can create interesting story people and can weave exciting predicaments occurring in unusual settings may still fail to grasp the magic blend because of bad timing. The writer who puts his hero in a scary situation before providing us with clues about the secret passage out of the dungeon or before he tells us of the short shelf life of the poison the hero has just consumed has lost touch with the importance of timing. These situations are no better than calling in the cavalry. These quick solutions become weeds that must be rooted out. The most effective writing tool for ridding your stories of these weeds is to time the planting of seeds to foreshadow the ending as your reader watches. He will not feel cheated at the end because you have concealed nothing from him.[13]

8

Methods of Characterization

Character is the most consequential element of prose fiction; magic arrives through characterizations. Without character and conflict, little remains for us to get excited about.

Story analysis reveals the methods writers have used to create real-life people with whom you and I can identify. Some methods are familiar. Others, while they are more complex, are not difficult and offer interesting approaches to characterization.

Methods

1. The author tells us:

> At sixteen, Joey Dimond was already an incorrigible liar.

2. A character reveals his nature each time his thoughts are opened to us:

I've been at it since I was nine . . . stealin' and lyin' about it. Kids always askin' me about it. "Why'd you do it, Joey?"

I ain't never been able to answer 'em. It's like somethin' inside makes me do it. How you gonna get a bunch of kids to understand somethin' like that. I coulda told 'em I needed the bread. Kids. Just snickered and grinned. I coulda told 'em anything.

3. Other characters tell us.

"Joey is a liar and a thief. We all know that. He learned to survive. But do you know that he's a sensitive, loving boy? He can't stand to hear a baby cry. After Mama left, I asked him to come live with me. He didn't want to, but I needed him to help me watch after the baby. I work late. But Joey's proud. He just came over when I needed him to baby-sit. My little girl just grew on him and he started staying over a few days, until he finally quit going back to the old place. Joey's proud, but he's smart. He took the necklace back and promised to pay for the broken window. And you know what? The man offered Joey a job."

4. A character's actions tell us.

On my left and my right, red and green neon signs flashed at the entrances to the bars and loan offices on both sides of Sixth Street. I huddled there in the dark alley. My knees were shakin' from the cold and from thinkin' of what I was about to do.

I heard the timid cry of a small kitten. It brushed my trouser leg. I pushed it aside, liftin' it gently with the toe of my shoe. Just a tiny thing. I hardly felt the weight of it.

The street was clear now. The jeweler's lighted showcase window was on my left. I moved in close, feelin' the cold iron crowbar in my hand. Off to my right, inside the ugly brick front, a jukebox started playin' a sad song.

> I raised the crowbar above my head and came down hard against the showcase window. Glass splintered and crashed around me. The alarm went off, clangin' and whoopin' loud enough to drown out the sad songs on the jukebox.
>
> I snatched the chain and the little heart with the diamond in the center and raced for the alley.
>
> The light from the street lamp lit up two tiny eyes, a weird mixture of pale green and grey . . . like the lights had gone on inside of them. I reached down and pulled the furry little beggar from the cold. Unzipped my jacket and dropped it inside. Felt my body drain its cold. . . .

5. Motives and reactions tell us. Motivation is the cause or reason for doing anything. What motivates one character will not move another to act. How our characters act or react to certain stimuli are factors we must know about them. Sometimes characters in stories seem to behave unreasonably, a common occurrence in romance novels, especially. Still, you should find these actions are consistent with the characters' earlier behaviors and reactions.[1]

6. Some descriptions tell us. Descriptions sometimes reveal more than just an outward appearance. For example, the narrator might describe a scene that sharply contrasts with what was described earlier or with what is expected. The description is thus revealing in itself.[2]

> Those who had before known her and had expected to behold her dimmed and obscured by a disastrous cloud, were astonished, and even startled, to perceive how her beauty shone out and made a halo of the misfortune and ignominy in which she was enveloped. It may be true that, to a sensitive observer, there was something exquisitely painful in it. (Nathaniel Hawthorne, *The Scarlet Letter*)

This description tells us that Hester Prynne is no ordinary woman. She appears in the light of day, coming forth from her prison, and the Puritan bystanders are startled by an appearance contrary to what they expected to see. Instead of appearing worn and defeated, cowering and ashamed, Hester Prynne appears more beautiful than ever. We get a glimpse of pride and strength of character as she wears her letter as something "exquisitely painful."

7. Descriptions of an implied past tell us.[3]

> Marty scrawled his signature and shoved the check under the metal grill. The teller finished posting some previous business and finally looked up. She parted her lips as if to say something.
>
> She didn't.
>
> He caught that queer look as it snapped from behind a pair of dark brown, bovine eyes. He saw it freeze there for a second. Then she turned casually as though she were exercising her neck, her eyes darting here and there at one clerk and then another; she licked her lips and swallowed hard.
>
> He caught his breath as slender, red-nailed fingers reached for his check. She didn't look at him, just held it close, examining it coldly. She turned it over and checked his endorsement.
>
> The eyes . . . he remembered those. She was the girl who had seen it happen.
>
> Marty felt the cold waves of terror. He shifted his weight on one foot, looked around him, his eyes darting first to the door and then to the small vice-president's office on his right. An armed guard moved toward the entrance.
>
> The woman counted the bills and pushed them under the glass shield. This time Marty was certain she was interested in the tiny scar just an inch under his left eye. He grabbed the bills without counting them, stuffed them into his pocket. How long

> would it take for her to remember what had happened?
> He glanced furtively about him, holding his breath. Then he moved abruptly, pressing toward the exit.

The reader gets only a glimpse into Marty's past. You don't know what Marty and the bank teller know, but there is a strong implication of a past that is about to catch up with our protagonist. Yet, we are still with Marty in the present; we haven't resorted to the flashback. We haven't stopped the forward movement of the story.

8. A word, a look, or a move can tell us:[4]

> "Open up!" The voice was gruff and demanding.
> Two men were seated near the pot-bellied stove in the center of the store. Their eyes cut immediately to the trader's son, seated nearest the door.
> The boy's eyes locked on his father, a tall, lean man behind the counter. The man lifted a shotgun from the wall rack and placed it gently on the counter.
> Across the room, near the back wall, a long-eared hound raised his head and sniffed the air. He whimpered. Groaned. Got up and disappeared behind the counter.
> The trader nodded to his son.

We have not yet identified the figure at the door. Still, strong clues about character have been provided by the reactions of those in the room. Even the hound signals to us. Has the animal suffered at the hands of the figure beyond the door?

Character or Plot Emphasis?

Many writers consider characterization the most important element in writing successful stories. This emphasis is not surprising, for character is developed through thoughts and desires, expressed or implied, and is inescapably related to the events that motivate the individual to act and react. Resistance is the tool that brings the protagonist's inner self into the open. Characterization and plot are thus inseparable.

When you are certain you understand the methods of characterization presented here, examine various stories and determinine what characterization methods are used. Remember that some of these are often overlooked, especially characterizations derived through selective descriptions and from settings. As a student, your serious investigation of these methods will greatly assure your success in story analysis. As a beginning writer, skillful applications of them will provide you with a major source of writing magic.

Remember: "Fiction is people."[5] Get to know them.

9

Atmosphere: Action, Mood, and Setting

What is happening, *where* it is happening, *when* it is happening, and the *mood* of each of these are the details for grasping the visual and emotional experiences intended by the authors. The writer blends the sensory images we derive from the story's action, mood, and setting. These three descriptive areas—action, mood, and setting—comprise our third key element, *atmosphere*.

The plot of your story is the frame; atmosphere is the flesh for that frame, supplying the mental pictures of the characters—characters motivated to act and react within skillfully designed patterns. Patterns of beauty and ugliness, innocence and guilt, and a variety of contrasting, emotional experiences are introduced to elicit the readers' interests and to assure their satisfaction. Our senses are stimulated with these experiences, and we are able to identify with what is real and with what the writer has intentionally implied.

Emotions Reflect Importance

Readers pay close attention to any reaction a character may have regarding a particular incident. How he reacts lets us know immediately just how important that incident is to the plot. We expect to share more exciting moments that expand and extend into other situations; the initial action now becomes a catalyst which eventually leads us to some greater critical point. This point may become a minor crisis, or it may actually signal a major crisis or the climax itself. If, however, the writer has overdramatized the emotional setting, we will quickly lose interest in the the story.

Emotions are constructed from carefully selected images planted in the setting, even before the character is sharply identified. The scene may contain no critical incident or problem. Although the emotion does not become as intense as when a crisis is included, it can and often does exist with carefully selected images.[1]

> He needed a cup of coffee. He pushed the car door open and forced his body out by sheer force of will. The Silver Moon Cafe was a dull replica of the ten others he had stopped at for coffee to stay awake. He had been too miserable to eat. From the looks of the place, he would be wiser not to eat. He crossed the frozen, snow-covered parking area. There were only two cars in the parking spaces. He was only slightly relieved. Probably belonged to the owners or workers. At least he wouldn't be forced to listen to customers bore him with their chatter about the weather.
>
> He glanced upward for a second and felt the miserable cold mist settle upon his face. Even the stars were sparkling fragments of ice in a dreary, black sky that sent waves of an ice-water coldness coursing through his veins.

He paused at the drab entrance. He peeked inside, but his view was blurred by the messy splotches and streaks of Christmas glitter and a poorly drafted Merry Christmas that had now become a dingy gray script against the sparsely lighted interior.

He entered with misgivings, letting his eyes move slowly about the room and its contents. A lone waitress dropped a coin in the jukebox. The scent of greasy bacon and sausages nauseated him. Behind the counter a short order cook was scrambling eggs and grilling sausages. The monotonous sounds of music and tiresome holiday lyrics pulsed from the jukebox.

"Merry Christmas!" the waitress called. "What'll you have?"

"Coffee," he said, and strained his eyes to find an empty table in the gloomy far corner.

Once he had tasted the coffee and his eyes had become accustomed to the semi-darkness, he saw there were two other middle-aged customers seated around tables that had been pulled together. The eggs and sausages were for them, he decided. He avoided meeting their glances, for he did not wish to converse with anyone. As soon as he finished his coffee, he would get back to the dreaded journey ahead of him.

The man is miserable, and his misery colors the café, the Christmas decorations at the entrance, the music from the jukebox, and the people inside, with gloom. Everybody knows people like this. They find gloom where others who have not been blinded or prejudiced by their own negative feelings find magic and beauty. If we allowed them to, they would spread their gloom into our own lives.

Still, these descriptions are essential for capturing the mood of our protagonist. The reader understands the effects specific problems will have upon him. From his behavior, we gauge the emotional pitch of the scene. Whatever happens now will probably bring the man additional suffering, until he manages to realize where his behavior is taking him.

Let's paint a different emotional setting for the same scene:

> He needed a cup of coffee to stay awake. He pushed the door open and broke from the car, standing to fill his lungs with the brisk December air. The Silver Moon Cafe was a quaint shop, sitting on a white sheet of snow. He looked up and felt the cool mist on his face, lifting his spirits as he made a wish upon the stars blinking merrily in a sky of black velvet.
>
> He read the Christmas greetings on the door and anticipated a pleasant hour with humble country folks like those who were waiting for him back home. He stepped inside and let his eyes adjust to the cozy atmosphere.
>
> "Merry Christmas!" someone called.
>
> He turned to see the waitress drop a coin in the jukebox. In seconds, the season's festive spirit rose and bubbled inside him as the simple holiday lyrics reminded him of his wife and his precious son, who were awaiting his arrival in Plum Hollow.
>
> Two middle-aged couples had drawn two tables together and were smiling at him. "Merry Christmas!" he exclaimed. He sniffed the air and caught the delicious aromas of sausage, eggs, and fresh coffee.

Choices of descriptive details provide a setting and character charged with positive or negative emotions. You decide which you want and develop it.

Planning Your Scenes

Before you write your scenes, do some planning. What emotions do you want to reveal? How much of the plot do you want to unravel before moving on to the next scene? Planning the extent and purposes of your scenes will help you organize their content and prevent "story sag" which often occurs in the middle.[2]

At one time, writers were encouraged to plot so that a character in an excited or tense mood at the beginning appeared to be less so at the end of the scene and vice versa. The scenes were then ordered so that a high-low scene followed a low-high scene. Recently, this approach has changed considerably. Writers maintain a certain mood level throughout the scene, heightening or lowering levels of tension to provide contrasts as needed. Still, students may find the rule helpful when revising their stories, especially when the middle portion offers problems. You can often save a floundering story by applying this old rule.[3]

The Setting

The *setting* of your story is its time and place. Three types of setting are written into stories, and either of these may be more important than the others.

Scenic Setting

Scenic setting is often no more than a glimpse of the specific scene where action is taking place. The writer may sometimes place casual descriptions at selected points; these are not always important for following the plot. You might mention whether it is night or day, whether the streets are busy or deserted, and a subtle mood will be felt by your characters in that setting. You may or may not return to the scene again during the length of that short story or novel.[4]

The following excerpt from George Harmon Coxe's mystery novel, *The Big Gamble,* illustrates the uses of small doses of scenic setting to keep the reader apprised of changing scenes as the action gets underway. Murdock has taken some pictures of a motor accident and is approached by a blonde who needs a lift. Later, she asks him to stop and get her some cigarettes. He tells her he has some, but she insists she will have to stop and get some anyway. She gives him some change. Murdock stops at a roadside diner:

> He got the cigarettes and matches from the tray and turned to the door, paying no attention to the half dozen customers at the counter. He got the door opened and started down the steps; then he stopped, staring open-mouthed at the spot where he had left the car.
>
> For the space was empty. . . . Then, cursing softly, he stepped to the ground and moved on out to the highway. A hundred yards away the main street opened up before him. . . . He started walking. . . .
>
> He strode along the sidewalk dodging the Saturday night shoppers and their children. Three blocks ahead was the police station.
>
> (George Harmon Coxe, *The Big Gamble,* Alfred A. Knopf, 1958, pp. 10, 11. Used by permission of the publisher and Brandt and Brandt)

The descriptive details provide us with enough images to set our minds in motion. We see more than the brief descriptions the author has given us, for we pull on our own mental reservoir of color, space, time, and emotion, which is immediately activated by the author's sensory details. We add to those lines, the color and emotional reactions that give the printed page a reason for being, the focus and tone the writer has intended to create.

Small doses of scenic setting work wonders for your readers. They experience an expanded imagery of city streets, automobile accidents, people in distress, and we are able to draw upon these experiences to fill in and complete the setting, mood, and action. Too many details clutter the scene and digress from the main intent of the writer: to disclose the *where,* the *how,* and the *what* of each situation while keeping the plot moving forward at a good pace.

Essential Setting

Stories with *essential settings* are those that could not have been set anywhere else, because their plots rely upon that specific time and place. It is difficult to imagine Hawthorne's *The Scarlet Letter* in a setting other than a Puritan New England community.[5]

Consider the essential nature of time and place in the opening paragraph from "The Sniper," by Liam O'Flaherty. In this opener, the author draws specific images of time and place where, though the story is fiction, similar events actually occurred during the 1920s; during this period, Dublin, the capital, was the setting for a civil war between Irish Republicans and Irish Free-Staters.

Let's examine the details of the opening paragraph:

1. Dublin lies in darkness, until the approaching dawn begins "casting a pale light over the streets and the dark waters of the Liffey."

2. The sound of heavy guns roar around the battered section known as "Four Courts."

3. The sounds of machine guns and rifles firing break spasmodically into the silence of night.

4. Republicans and Free-Staters are involved.

If we've studied our history, we know this story is based in Ireland in the 1920s. Many of us are not as familiar with Ireland's capital city, Dublin, as we are with Rome, Paris, Tokyo, and other cities. But Dublin becomes an essential setting for this fictionalized version of what happened there.

We can easily decide whether a setting is essential or familiar by asking ourselves a few questions: Could the story have taken place anywhere else, or does the setting charm us with memorable experiences of a universally recognized location?

Your setting will determine the scope, the accuracy, or the universal charm your descriptive details will offer the reader. Essential settings depend upon descriptive references based upon what actually happened in that specific time and place. At the same time, the essential setting may also become a familiar setting if the reader perceives a number of images of people at work and play.

Familiar Settings

How many times have you been drawn to a magazine story from the artist's illustration of a *familiar setting?* These are often places we visit, read about, or see in films and newsreels: a New England fishing village, the icy tundra of Siberia, the quaint street cafes in Paris, the foggy streets of London, and the wharves of Liverpool. Here in The United States, we enjoy Niagara Falls, Shenandoah, and Key Largo, and, while down in New Orleans, The French Quarter with its Bourbon Street. These familiar settings have been used often and will be used again; their use guarantees instant mental images for readers drawn to familiar settings, even when the plot and characters are commonplace.[6]

Setting and Character

Once you have established a good background for a novel, you will often be able to imagine human situations developing there. First, however, you must know your characters inside and out, and you must decide upon the immediate objectives your protagonist has in mind in order to choose a specific setting from that background. If your choice is right, your vivid impressions of that familiar setting will generate spontaneous, fresh, and exciting ideas you will need to motivate and enhance the actions of your protagonist. Obviously, a writer must also have strong impressions of the various settings that make up a novel's background before a protagonist can respond with his/her best performance in every instance. Getting the most from your background takes work and time, but once you allow your characters to be stirred by their surroundings, their characterization is more effective.[7]

Atmosphere and Your Chosen Genre

In the short story, economy in every phase of the story's development is essential. Blending the three elements of atmosphere—action, mood and setting—is many times the means for achieving this economy. The length dictates an economy of descriptive words and phrases, necessitating exact word choices for every facet of your story's construction. In the novel, the writer can explore each of these three ingredients separately. The setting may be described with intricate details, providing a mood suitable for the action about to take place. Eventually, characters are brought into the setting, completing the staging for significant action.

Atmosphere and character blend naturally. It is not easy to talk about one without including the other. Characters poke around in dark corners, descend into dangerous pits, fight their way through rapids or through angry crowds, and wait out violent storms, holed up like animals in the corner of barns. We are made to see, to hear, to taste, to smell, and to touch or feel whatever the characters are experiencing. From these perceptions, we discover clear aspects of character.

What might these perceptions reveal to us?

1. They might tell us what a character will endure to reach a goal.

2. They might reveal that he is selfish, concerned only for his own safety.

3. They might reveal courage and compassion, or the opposite of these.

4. They might uncover a hidden motive for actions.

5. They might exhibit dangerous signs of self-destruction.

6. They might uncover hidden talents, intellect, or charm.

In Chapter 8, you learned how character can be drawn from descriptive setting, action, and mood. Though you were unable to see, the reactions of the characters inside the trading post revealed what the person beyond the door must be like. Strong, visual emotions from within the setting, including those of the hound, gave importance to the character beyond the door.

Atmosphere alone can greatly impact every scene you build. Examine the novels of John Steinbeck for the rich tapestries of description he has woven to characterize individuals, and to create sharp sensory images within carefully plotted elements of time, space, and order of importance. You will sense the magic, and you will begin to recognize the full power of description to create real-to-life people, settings, and deeds.

Follow Up

Read "By the Waters of Babylon," by Stephen Vincent Benét. The entire story is clothed in rich descriptive atmosphere, which becomes the dominant element of that narrative.

Reread this chapter. Find examples from the story that illustrate the setting, the action, and the mood. Do these change? Locate descriptions that characterize individuals. In what instances does atmosphere bring out the worst or the best in an individual's character?

10

Methods for Presenting the Setting

Four methods for presenting your setting will be explored here: (1) through description, (2) through dialogue, (3) through the use of symbols, and (4) through the use of historical backgrounds. The two used most often are description and dialogue.

Setting by Description

The experienced writer uses three methods for describing objects, people, landscapes, action, and moods within the setting. These three methods are: time order, space order, and order of importance. You will probably recognize these devices as transitional words, sentences, and whole paragraphs on the movements of your protagonist and other figures in the setting. Choice descriptions provide images that will carry your reader along with your roving camera eye, moving from point to point.

How the transition is effected between scenes should be observed carefully, for it is at these strategic points that the beginning writer often loses his readers. The reader finds himself stopping and reading a passage again to determine what went wrong and to try to mend the broken connection. If he is unable to make the proper connection, the story suffers.

Time Order

It's impossible to write a novel that ignores time. When your novel begins, time starts ticking away. Characters can only come alive through motion and the passing of time, each situation unfolding at a pace that is suitable for the event's importance. The novelist works constantly with *time and place*. Place, of course, is passive. Time becomes the mover. The passing of time brings forth the action; it is the instrument of change. "If time should break down, the novel itself would lie in collapse, its meaning gone. For time has the closest possible connection with the novel's meaning, in being the chief conductor of the plot."[1]

Time, like space, is almost palpable when we write of night, morning, afternoon, but what the writer should be most concerned with is the time falling between these periods of the day. An author can take us back in time to a dozen different places, but the time it takes for the character to get us there and bring us home again must be accounted for.[2]

Time Elements: Flashbacks and Transitions

Two elements—*flashbacks and transitions*—are involved with the passage of time, and they must eventually be dealt with in creating fiction. The two can become troublesome. Difficulties are especially frequent for beginners who have not yet become fully aware of the mechanics involved in the development of either element and the pitfalls that are sometimes encountered. Transitions must precede and follow the flashback as well as keep the reader apprised of movement from scene to scene. The entire process must include a measurement of the passing of time.[3]

When should a flashback be used? How do you move back and forth in time without losing your reader's interest? When should flashbacks be avoided altogether?

Some writers argue that flashbacks should not be used in the short story, but there are exceptions to everything. Again, we sometimes find them necessary for dramatizing an important event and for avoiding long expositions or dull "rememberings." How easy it would be if we could plunge into action and keep slugging it out, scene after scene, nonstop, to the end! But prior events have brought the characters to their present plight, and the reader must grasp them before the story can make good sense. "There are always going to be *who, what, when, where* and *why* to consider. It is the more complicated *why* that gives us trouble."[4]

Expositional passages in short stories are quite common for providing brief, substantive flashbacks—those having genuine purposes. The following excerpt was taken from "Miss Brill," a short story by Katherine Mansfield. Her story pattern and writing style are especially suited to the flashback. The drifting, streams-of-consciousness style are in the fashion of Virginia Woolf, the novelist, whose works—including her diaries and short stories—are valuable lessons in imagery, mood, and writer discipline.

Miss Brill has been observing the people gathering to listen to the music in the park. Her spirits are high as she listens while pretending not to listen, as she sees while pretending not to see. She considers herself quite an expert in other people's lives as they sit and talk beside her. She notices two old people seated beside her now, sharing her special park bench. One is a man in a velvet coat, holding a carved walking stick. Beside him is an old woman with a roll of knitting in her lap.

> She glanced sideways at the old couple. Perhaps they would go soon. [Now we are taken back in time] Last Sunday, too, hadn't been as interesting as usual. An Englishman and his wife, he wearing a dreadful Panama hat and she button boots. And she'd gone on the whole time about how she ought to wear spectacles; she knew she needed them; but that it was no good getting any; they'd be sure to break and they'd never keep on. And he'd been so patient. He'd suggested everything—gold rims, the kind that curved round your ears, little pads inside the bridge. No, nothing would please her. "They'll always be sliding down my nose!" Miss Brill had wanted to shake her.
>
> [Now we are brought back to the present]
>
> The old couple sat on the bench, still as statues. Never mind, there was always the crowd to watch. . . . (Katherine Mansfield, *The Short Stories of Katherine Mansfield*, 1922. Used by permission of Alfred A. Knopf, Inc.)

Miss Brill's thoughts reflect her changing spirit—gentle, abrasive, selfish, or bright, as it may be for brief periods. Character is developed from her reactions to the visual and emotional stimuli surrounding her.

You will usually find flashbacks toward the beginning of novels. The story begins with action that gets the plot off to a good start, building the reader's interest in what is happening to the protagonist. Once our interest is hooked, a smooth transition takes us into a flashback, introducing an incident that further illuminates our lead character and provides him with certain traits and skills that allow later feats to be more realistic.[5]

The flashback might include one or more complete chapters before bringing us back to the present, while others can be as brief as the one in "Miss Brill." Keep your readers in mind. Do not lose them in a lengthy flashback that might allow them to forget what has come before. The best security against this danger is in making certain that your lead characters and the opening action have become solidly impressed upon the readers' minds before any flashback occurs.

Too Much Information

Phyllis Whitney, prolific author of many books for adults and young people alike, offers some cogent advice in her *Guide to Fiction Writing*. She warns about including too much information in the transitional passages between scenes. In other words, do not allow nonessential material to clutter up the transition. Sometimes all you would have to do is add few extra spaces after your scene ends, indent, and start a new scene.[6]

To illustrate:

> Jen looked at his watch. Nine-twenty. "How long will it take?"
>
> "Airport or bus terminal?" The cab driver started the engine.
>
> "Airport!"
>
> "Traffic's heavy. Twenty minutes."
>
> "Let's go!"
>
> Overhead, Jen heard a huge jetliner approaching the far end of the brightly lighted runway. He looked up. A cool night mist

dampened his face. There were few stars. He straightened up, glancing back at the great wall clock visible inside the terminal. Nine-forty.

Just in time, he thought. He fidgeted with the plain gold band on his finger.

In the first scene, the exact time is noted. In the first paragraph of the next scene, we learn that it is the same night, twenty minutes later. Note that the transitional space does not interrupt the narrative flow.

Spacing between scenes isn't always necessary. The spaces weren't absolutely necessary in Jen's story, though it does give an immediate signal to the reader to get ready for a change in the action and, possibly, the setting. At other times, exposition paragraphs are needed before the author can take us into a new scene. In either case, time must be accounted for.

Space Order

The eyes of the storyteller search the scene. A person, a landscape, and any objects of significance inside that particular setting are seen from a specific viewpoint. Where does the storyteller begin his visual interpretation? How does he provide us with the verbal arrows that allow us to follow the movement of a person, to sense not only the timeliness but the spacial relationships between people and objects? How far have the eyes of the narrator traveled since the action started rolling? How did he manage to get us inside the house? To the bedroom where the body was first discovered? Time is evident here, too, but we are now concentrating on the descriptions that provide imagery of space: depth and height, width and breadth, outside, inside, above and below.

We follow each movement of the storyteller's eye, for his eyes are our eyes. They report on what is essential and on how each part of the setting is unique. Without their perceptions, we are blind.

Order of Importance

The *order of importance* is sometimes the order in which events occur. At other times, the writer decides which descriptions, and of what, should be handled first. Usually authors describe the least important objects and work toward the more significant objects in the setting.

Descriptive Setting in the Novel

The Grapes of Wrath, by John Steinbeck, is an important novel for study by students and writers. In Chapter 1, powerful descriptive passages clearly illustrate the three methods for developing descriptive settings; also, the author uses the descriptive setting and the conflict it imposes to characterize nature as an antagonist.

First, let's examine the opening paragraph of Chapter 1:

> To the red country and part of the gray country of Oklahoma, the last rains came gently, and they did not cut the scarred earth. The plows crossed and recrossed the rivulet marks. The last rains lifted the corn quickly and scattered weed colonies and grass along the sides of the roads so that the gray country and the dark red country began to disappear under a green cover. In the last part of May the sky grew pale and clouds that had hung in high puffs for so long in the spring were dissipated. The sun flared down on the growing corn day after day until a line of brown spread along the edge of each green bayonet. The clouds appeared, and went away, and in a

> while they did not try anymore. The weeds grew darker green to protect themselves, and they did not spread any more. The surface of the earth crusted, a thin hard crust, and the sky became pale, so the earth became pale, pink in the red country and white in the gray country. (John Steinbeck, *The Grapes of Wrath*. Penguin Books, 1981, p. 1. Used by permission of Penguin Books USA, Inc.)

The novel begins by describing a problem that becomes more threatening as the chapter continues. Nature is becoming an antagonist. How does Steinbeck describe the changes that occur?

First, he contrasts between two areas of Oklahoma—the red country and the gray country. He notes that the rain ends just as the corn is shooting upward from the earth and the weeds are covering the area, reducing the contrast, turning the land green. Time is apparent in the changes on the land and its vegetation.

How does he handle space? He begins with the broad description of the two colors of the Oklahoma land areas. He notes the effect of little and then no rain at all. He moves his camera-eye upward to a changing sky and brings us back to the land where the sun's rays have changed the colors. The land becomes first one color, green, but then changes as the weeds stop growing, and the land hardens into a crust. The third person narrator then takes us back to a sky that has grown pale. Finally, he tells us that the red country has become pink, and the gray country has become white. He ends where he began, all in one paragraph. His descriptions account for time—it is the month of May at the midpoint of the paragraph—and he has taken us from earth to sky to earth to sky in one brief passage.

As the chapter continues, the importance of the gradual destruction of the land is identified. Finally nature reaches inside the houses, settling as dust that has filtered through the cracks in the walls. *Time and space descriptions* continue to unravel before us, full-circle, including threatening changes in the earth and in the sky.

Toward the end of the chapter, we observe the behavior of the people who come out of their houses to assess the damages wrought by nature. Through description, these people are characterized by their actions and their quiet anger and resolve.

Time Order

The time covered in this first chapter is approximately two months, beginning in mid-April and ending in mid-June. How does Steinbeck fill in this time? He reveals the many changes that come over the land when the rain slows and then stops completely. Each step thereafter is marked by changes on earth and in the sky—in the fields, along the roadsides, in the air, in the sun, and in the homes. As he shifts from one spot to another, the author deals with elements of *space order*. He has also moved from the start of the problem and has carried us through to the most critical point—what will the people do next?

Space Order and Order of Importance

We ought now to give special attention to the last paragraph in the chapter, where selected details provide characterizations: Men move out of their houses; children move out of the houses; men stand by their fences; eyes move to the fields; women move out of the houses to stand beside their husbands; children observe their parents and turn their faces away when noticed; horses move to the watering troughs; faces of the men become "hard and angry and resistant"; the feelings of the women observed; the feelings of the children are observed; women move back into their houses to work; children begin to play; time is registered in clearing skies and a sun that becomes less red; the men move to the doorway of their houses; they sit still—"thinking and figuring."

Here Steinbeck has used descriptions to characterize the men and women by their actions and reactions during a moment of crisis. The children are characterized as well. These are people who have known hardships before. They look into each others' faces and know that everything will be all right. The men have not been broken. The children feel the agony of the ordeal; they reveal it in their cautious play and in the way they avoid being caught looking on when their parents stand close together examining the damage.

Tone and Foreshadowing

The purpose of the first chapter is to set the *tone* of the novel, to characterize the great natural antagonism that forces the "Okies" to move west in search of a better life. Steinbeck also characterizes the people here, who appear strong, hopeful, and determined. As we follow them on the long journey to California, Steinbeck foreshadows even greater trials ahead for them. When they are faced with the heavy burdens in the "promised land," then, their behavior is credible, for we have learned who and what these people are.

Essential Settings

Today, since we now look back upon that period, Steinbeck's novel is an historical record. The settings, first

Oklahoma, then the long journey west, and finally the camps of the sickly, displaced, suffering humanity near the vineyards of California, are essential. The events did not happen and probably could not have happened anywhere else.

Using Dialogues

Effective *dialogues* offer writers an opportunity to break long narrative portions of the text. In fact, one purpose of dialogue is to introduce a setting devoid of such long narrative passages. Conflict introduced in conversation is far more effective than a description of rising problems. When characters speak, we should be able to uncover not only character, but additional plot elements as well.

How many plot elements does the dialogue contain in the following incident?

> Josh crossed the service road behind his house and stepped upon the patio. He stopped to pick the sandspurs from his sneakers and bluejeans.
>
> "That a buzzard?" Carmella, the housekeeper, parted the screen door and stepped onto the patio.
>
> Josh straightened up. A hawk circled the field of tall grasses behind the house. "Naw, a Cooper's hawk."
>
> "He eat chickens?" She twisted the wire seal on a trash bag and crossed the concrete patio to the incinerator, lifted the top, and deposited the trash.
>
> "I don't know. Littl'ns, maybe."
>
> "He see somethin' out there, Josh." She reached for the broom handle she used to loosen the trash for quick burning.
>
> "Where?" He saw the smoke rise from the stack and hang low as it moved up and outwards across the fields.
>
> The woman brushed her mouth nervously with a forefinger. "There! Somethin' moving out there in the grass."

"Charlie? I think it's Charlie!"

"Who's Charlie?"

A restless night and the nightmare had left him tense. Charlie had been in the dream. He'd been trapped at the bottom of a six foot grave. . . .

"Charlie who, Josh!"

"Charlie, that crazy owl from Mockingbird Branch."

"Owls come out nights, Josh. Everybody know that."

"He's starved, Carmella. They come out when they're hungry."

"That hawk gonna git 'im."

"The field's his territory during the day."

Josh felt the roots of his blond hair tingle. He moved out toward the field.

Carmella was shaken by his sudden move. "Wait, Josh! Maybe . . . ."

And he looked down into the open grave. Charlie was there in the darkness, limp and wretched. Josh reached down to pull him to safety and saw the large rattlesnake, coiled at the opposite end, poised to strike. . . .

But Josh appeared to be moved by some powerful force.

She started out behind him, but after only a few yards into the field, her heavy weight taxed her breathing. She halted to catch her breath, complained of sandspurs that stuck to her socks and pricked her legs and ankles.

"Go back!" Josh warned. "They get worse!"

He stopped. The owl was less than a hundred feet in front of him. "It's Charlie. He's caught a mouse."

Josh looked up. The hawk can see Charlie, too, he decides. Had he seen the mouse Charlie claimed in the hawk's territory?

The grasses moved in front of Josh.

The hawk must have seen the movement in the last full second of his dive, for he pulled his head back, flapped his wings with hard thrusts and drew his limbs up snug with his body as though escaping some dreadful encounter.

Josh saw the rattler, too. All five, diamond-backed feet of him. Less than three feet away, Charlie held on to his tiny field mouse and tried to get aloft. He bounced forward a couple of feet, like a miniature kangaroo.

Josh feared something else—something he could not identify or explain.

Carmella groaned. "Here!" She handed Josh the broomstick. "Kill that reptile!"

"He's gonna strike!"

The woman grabbed a double handful of sand and threw it into the rattler's open jaws.

The snake struck. Missed. He was stretched out now, and more vulnerable, Josh thought. He came down hard with the jagged edges of the broom handle, piercing the soft spot behind the viper's head, pinning him to a clump of crabgrass. He put more weight on the stick and held fast. The rattler began wrapping his thick body around the stick.

Carmella, breathing hard, came down upon the snake's head with a heavy heel, severed the head from the body. She stepped back. "He won't get no deader, I reckon."

And he closed his eyes to erase what he saw. When he opened them again, he marveled at his success. Charlie and the snake had disappeared from the grave!

"Everything all right, Josh?"

"Huh? Aw, yeah. Let's go."

Josh looked around for Charlie and found the owl enjoying his lunch, perched on a low branch of a persimmon tree.

The hawk had disappeared.

Josh started back toward the house, slowly this time so the housekeeper could keep up.

"It's gonna rain," Carmella said.

"So?"

"We gotta burn that snake," she said.

"Naw, let it be," Josh said.

"You just crossed that spot when . . . when you come back to the house."

"So?" He hadn't told anybody about his dream. He began to think now that maybe he should have. Sometimes, if you talk about something playing heavy on your mind, it doesn't seem as important.

"I seen your footprints in the sand," she said.

"So?" He felt a chill creep over his spine.

He looked down into the dark grave a second time. This time he looked into the dark eyes of his friend, Jen Roman. Jen's arm had been bloodied. . . . A familiar voice called to Josh from the fire tower—a shrill, hysterical voice, "Bury him, Josh. Bury him! Bury him now before it's too late!"

"Don't you worry, Josh. I'll burn a black candle."

But he does worry. Is Jen in trouble?

He felt the cool raindrops on his face and looked up. The sky was rapidly becoming dark and scary.

How many plot elements were you able to find? (See the last section of this chapter for answers to this question).

Symbolic Settings

When the writer uses some familiar object—a moon, a tide, a cross to represent something else in the story, we call it a *symbol*. Symbols are used for a number of purposes, each defined and explained fully in Chapter 17. A symbol in the setting—the ocean's tide, for example—serves several purposes: to parallel plot events, to accent a theme, or for other purposes explained later. This incident is called a symbolic incident, with references to several symbols first encountered in the nightmare, presented as the "Prologue" to the novel,

Summer of the Owl. These and other references to the owl, the hawk, the rattlesnake, and the grave—all symbols having clear purposes—represent frightening and frustrating events occurring in that novel.

Historical Settings

Stories woven around historical settings involving ministers of state, generals on the battlefield, and characters representing real events in the past require a certain amount of research to describe accurately the scenes, action, and conflict. Costumes, manners, and speech must conform to the time and place and to the prevailing customs. Each must be accurately presented or your readers will protest.

Follow-Up

The *fictional incident* in this chapter includes many structural and supportive plot elements: atmosphere is found in the action, the mood, and the setting. The setting extends from the patio behind the house to the sandy, grassy field. Psychological flashbacks take us into Josh's nightmare experiences. Here we gather some of the references relating to symbolic importance in the setting. The mood is one of growing curiosity, quickly overshadowed by fear. Each detail of atmosphere is drawn from both the dialogue and the narrative descriptions tied to it.

Conflict is foreshadowed when we learn from the nightmare that Josh's best friend lies in a grave, his arm bloodied. The grave and reference to his friend would have little symbolic meaning if there had been no actual events that happened as they have in the dream. We expect Josh to find his friend in serious danger. This is a seed planted to generate suspense. At the same time, let's not forget the conflict in nature before them.

Character comes from what our characters say, think, and do, as well as from descriptions. Carmella is sensitive to what Josh says and what he does. We know from her behavior that she both respects and cares for Josh, who is sensitive and compassionate toward animals as well as toward his friend.

He's had a terrible nightmare that he can't forget. What happens in the field that afternoon continues the tension which should reach new levels and lead us to some satisfying conclusion.

You should be feeling some of the fun and excitement that can be had from plotting and analyzing stories and story people. The more you work at it, the more you will understand how significant and beneficial a writer's tools are.

11

Conflict: When Two Goals Collide

A fifth key element of prose fiction is conflict. When conflict begins, your story begins; when the conflict ends, your story ends. Somewhere between the beginning and the ending, your principal character must face one or more antagonist—man, nature, himself—who will present a series of challenges in conflict with his goals. These challenges must be clear and reasonable, and they must be resolved to the satisfaction of your readers.[1]

Conflict is linked directly to your story pattern or plot, for without it your characters are not given an opportunity to show us who and what they are. Each challenge your protagonist faces is plotted, beginning with a minor crisis of some sort. Your key character may solve the initial obstacle, only later to discover a bigger obstacle blocking his forward progress. Or, trying and failing to solve the initial problem, the matter becomes more complex, perhaps affecting your protagonist in any number of ways. He may begin to lose faith, and psychological conflict troubles him as well. By the time the climax is reached, your reader should be anxious to find out how the issue is resolved. If you have provided a credible ending, the reader will not feel cheated.

Beginners' Common Errors

Beginning writers often present their characters with one confrontation after another, apparently with little concern for the ending. This is especially counterproductive in the short story. The length does not allow time for wasted action; only those events important to the conclusion should be included.[2]

Readers are satisfied when two factors are realized in the end: a definite conclusion and inevitability. A *definite conclusion* is produced when the hero or heroine manages to resolve the problems, or—if the lead characters are unsympathetic—when they are soundly defeated. *Inevitability* is realized when the protagonist solves the problems in a credible manner.[3]

When you plot your short story, examine every incident to make certain that each becomes a logical action based upon what has previously occurred. For example, if your hero is trapped inside a room behind locked doors and does not have a key, examine previous information carefully before he suddenly comes up with a special device to help him pick the lock and free himself. Readers must be informed earlier of his skills in picking locks, and the wire must have been placed in his pockets for some other purpose during the course of the previous action. With this assurance, inevitability is achieved. Any illogical result, those not based upon consideration of previous action, produces an unacceptable ending readers will immediately reject.[4]

Protagonist vs. Antagonist

Though the *protagonist* is determined to reach his goals at any cost, the *antagonist* is equally determined to stop him. Your antagonist needs to be a full-bodied character as well, skillfully countering each move your principal figure makes. Readers relish this threatening element, applauding each victory your protagonist achieves.[5]

Your protagonist has been shaped with labor and love so that he executes the moves required to accomplish his goals; however, he should never do anything just because the plot requires it. His character cannot fluctuate like stock market prices.

When writers allow characters to do what the plot requires, the story suffers. Then, going back and characterizing the protagonist in line with their later actions becomes imperative. This problem can be avoided entirely, however, by carefully plotting each major segment of the story and making certain that the characters are developed substantially before the writing begins. In some instances, you will want to change the plot to accommodate your characters. Often, you will discover that certain characters are so strongly outlined in your mind that they begin moving in their own directions. They pull at the reins you hold; but hold tight to those reins, never allowing your protagonist or any other character to waste time doing things that do not lend themselves to the full development of the plot and its forward movement.

Open with a Crisis

All future action grows out of the *initial crisis,* which should occur in the opening of your story. Your protagonist is responsible for resolving that crisis. After this point, every scene must have a purpose, a problem, and a goal.[6] Difficulties continue to emerge as psychological, emotional, or physical obstacles are carefully placed in the paths of your principal characters. Purpose here means that your protagonist must attempt to resolve each problem he encounters in every scene, driving him or her into action and leading us into the next scene, and the next.[7]

Reader Identification

Because your story involves a character who has recognizable, realistic goals that press him toward an exciting and purposeful achievement, we readily identify with him. We sympathize with him as he forges violent rapids, as he climbs the dangerous, precipitous peaks to reach the one he loves. We cringe when he makes serious mistakes in judgment; we cheer him on when he learns from his mistakes but perseveres. Yet, the way ahead lies riddled with obstacles. The tension mounts. Though he is created from the seeds of imagination, we are made to feel that he is real.

Around and within him emerges the fires of ambition, greed, compassion, intuition, hunger, jealousy, curiosity, love, and hate. Any one of these fires is enough to set sparks flying in the right setting. A few words of warning, however: Do not build excitement and reader suspense only to have your protagonist solve his problem too quickly, not allowing him to overcome his difficulties through the use of his own brand of ingenuity and character.

Undeveloped Conflict

Suppose your principal character is caught in the midst of a terrible winter storm. He becomes snowbound with a friend who lies stricken with acute appendicitis. Whatever happens next must stem from the actions these two take to overcome the problem, or should stem from a past action that is linked with the current solution and gives it credibility.

Let's say the two start out with the sick man secured onto a dog sled. They quickly discover this step is doomed to failure as the snow quickly obscures the view. Puzzled by the loss of landmarks that may have guided them in the direction of safety, they ramble aimlessly, unable to reach their objective. Readers anticipate these problems, but they also expect sound plotting to drop clues along the way to explain the appearance of a rescue team, including a surgeon who performs an emergency appendectomy. Perhaps a trader dropped by the cabin earlier, before the man's condition became critical. He remembers that the two were planning to leave at daybreak for the village where the ailing man could get help. When the storm worsens, the trader acts. The reader can believe the explanation and not feel cheated. "The classic plot involves a steady worsening of the problem until at the peak of their conflict, they save themselves—or die trying."[8]

Motivation and Action

What a character chooses to do at any one time is sparked by *motivation,* his reason for doing anything. Internal motivation is derived from a character's own mind and heart. He acts in a particular way because some things make his blood boil and others make him withdraw. He may find himself penniless and hungry in a strange city; he may be lonely and afraid. But whatever situation, the kind of person he is will determine what action he will take. He acts and reacts to the tune inside of him and around him.

Characters can act according to both *internal and external motives*. Perhaps the motives are generated by the actions of others around him or by nature.

Fear is a very common emotion characters experience—often a physical fear but just as often other kinds of fear. Fear drives people to act. A good writer allows fears to change as the story develops, but continued fear of one thing slackens tension and bores the reader.[9] Change in a character is essential—either growth or deterioration—for realism demands change. The fears are real, and the mastery of them must come from actions and change in our protagonist.[10]

Characters must also be examined outside the bounds of the story's main thrusts. Each should have a past that has affected him, and readers should be allowed to see how this past has changed him. We may learn of deep concerns about the fate of others—a wife, girlfriend, son, or daughter— for whom a protagonist puts himself in physical, emotional, and spiritual jeopardy.[11]

Resolving Conflict

Finally, let's examine the six possible endings for resolving conflict as they are suggested by F. A. Rockwell in his *How to Write Plots that Sell:*[12]

1. The protagonist overcomes all obstacles.
2. The protagonist loses.
3. The protagonist and the antagonist win.
4. The protagonist and the antagonist lose.
5. The protagonist and the antagonist reach a compromise.

6. The protagonist wins but suffers a terrible loss of something or someone very important and dear to him.

Conflict and the Plot

In analyzing stories, you must decide who the characters are, what motivates the characters, and to what lengths they went to get what they wanted. What were the obstacles they overcame? What in the principal character's makeup especially fitted him for overcoming these obstacles? Were the obstacles formidable? Did fate enter the arena and make it too easy for the protagonist?

To get a firm grasp of how conflict is initiated and developed in the short story, let's analyze "The Sniper," by Liam O'Flaherty. Note the effect *irony* makes in forming a powerful, emotional conclusion. We can make our work easier, however, by first organizing an outline of this short story and examining the plot pattern to uncover elements of both conflict and irony.

I. Civil War rages in Dublin, Ireland
   A. June twilight fades into night
   B. Heavy guns, machine guns, and rifles fire
   C. Conflict between Republicans and Free-Staters

The opening paragraphs of short stories often prove to be the most difficult to write. Writers want to get us into the story's action as quickly as possible, preferably in the first sentence. How successful has this author been with his opener? He begins with descriptive atmosphere, obvious even in the outline (I). The setting, the mood, and the action are made clear to us—Civil War has come to the streets and rooftops of Dublin, Ireland.

II. Protagonist is a Republican sniper
   A. He looks down from a rooftop, toward O'Connell Bridge
      1. Young man, with eyes of a fanatic, of one used to looking at death
      2. Eats a sandwich and drinks some whiskey from a flask
      3. Contemplates the dangers of lighting and enjoying a cigarette.
   B. Light draws enemy sniper's fire.
      1. Republican peers over parapet
      2. Free-Stater fires from opposite side of street
      3. Republican moves to new position near chimney
      4. Sees only dim outline of opposite rooftop
      5. Decides enemy sniper under cover

Section II is the second phase of the introduction. The protagonist is identified and characterized through descriptive detail: eyes of a fanatic, used to looking at death, aware of dangers. War has made him hard and momentarily insensitive about preserving any life other than his own.

The minor crisis has not yet occurred. The Republican sniper is merely doing what he has been doing for days, weeks, or even months. In addition to characterization, the author has managed to describe the manner in which this war is being fought.

III. Enemy reinforced
   A. Armored car advances across the bridge
      1. Moves into the street and stops

        2. Republican sniper aware that his bullets are futile against armor
    B. An old woman informer points him out
        1. Enemy at turret looks up and is felled by sniper's bullet
        2. Informer hit and lies in gutter

The *minor crisis* appears when the armored car crosses the bridge and the Republican sniper is pointed out by a woman informer. While attempting to solve this crisis, his problem intensifies. Though he has been able to destroy the threat from the street, he has exposed his position on the roof to an enemy sniper located on the roof across the street.

IV. Enemy sniper on opposite roof retaliates
    A. Republican is wounded in arm
        1. Drops to roof and crawls back to parapet, unable to raise rifle
        2. Enduring the pain, cleans wound and dresses it
    B. Morning must find him off the roof
        1. Must kill the enemy
        2. Has only a revolver

In these few paragraphs (Section IV), rapid action and reaction leads to and formulates our *major crisis*. Our Republican sniper is wounded and unable to lift his rifle. The agony and fear that follow round out the major crisis. He must get off the roof before the morning light exposes him.

V. Republican sniper lays trap
    A. He draws the enemy's fire

1. Places cap over muzzle of rifle
2. Pushes rifle over parapet so cap is seen
3. Enemy fires, hits cap

B. He fools the enemy
1. Holds rifle in middle, lets his arm hang limply over parapet
2. Lets rifle fall into the streets below
3. Falls back limply upon the roof

C. He moves away to another position, unseen

In this section, the actions of our protagonist further characterize him as determined, intelligent, and cunning. Every step he takes is now motivated by his will to survive. Conflict continues to follow him as long as he feels trapped on the roof.

VI. Republican sniper springs trap

A. He sees enemy exposed on the rooftop
1. Republican sniper fires
2. Enemy hit
3. Enemy struggles to keep balance and falls to the street below

B. Republican feels differently about killing
1. Feels remorse
2. Feels revolt at the sight of the shattered body below
3. Curses the war, himself, and everybody
4. Throws revolver onto the roof
5. Explosion from revolver brings him back to his senses

Our major crisis continues to develop in this second major segment or body of the story. Note that the actions and reactions intensify. Something else takes place here, too. Our chief character has changed his attitude about killing. Can we believe that a man could change so sharply in the space of about one page or so? Yes, we can. In the beginning, atmosphere and characterization have shown him to be cold and insensitive. He killed the man in the armored car and the informer who pointed him out with little emotion. War had a cruel effect upon him.

We have seen the effects of the war in Vietnam upon the men who fought it and upon an entire nation that began to question our presence there. The stresses of jungle fighting led some men to experiment with drugs. A few were involved in horror stories of mass murders of innocent civilians. Public indignation swelled as the nation's conscience was aroused. A president chose not to run for a second term. Finally, the fighting was ended, but the bitter harvest will serve as a memorial to the futility of war for years to come.

We have followed the spiritual and psychological influences in the development of Henry Fleming, the protagonist in Stephen Crane's *The Red Badge of Courage*. Henry entered the war with a youth's romantic vision of soldiers on the move, involved in great battles. When the end came, his vision was that of a man who saw war as it really was—bloody and cruel. Now, reflecting upon these developments in fiction and nonfiction, we understand the powerful stresses of war and their effects upon man.

In realism, our characters must change. In the moment that follows the killing of his enemy, the sniper becomes aware of the splattered body of the enemy in the street below. The explosion in the chamber of his own pistol helps snap him out of his momentary coldness. We can believe that the beginning reflected his anxiety, the heightening of fear, and the need for self-preservation. The final scene on the rooftop represents the moment of awakening, when the stresses are relieved by a lessening of fear for his own life.

Important: Change must begin before the climax is underway. In "The Sniper," change is apparent now on the rooftop following the killing of the enemy when he has been shocked by an explosion from his own pistol. Does the author foreshadow any change earlier? Read this story and decide for yourself.

VII. As the smoke clears
  A. Decides to leave rooftop
    1. Finishes the flask of whiskey
    2. Decides to look for his commander
    3. Picks up his revolver and pockets it
    4. Crawls through the skylight and down to the street

This is the beginning of the ending, the rapid rise to the climax. From the outline, you can feel the return to an orderly turn of behavior that gives further evidence of psychological restoration.

VIII. Curious about enemy sniper
  A. Had he known the dead sniper?
    1. Decides sniper had been a good shot
    2. Had they once served together before the split in the army?
  B. Decides to go over and take a look
    1. Firing in other parts of the street
    2. Darted across street
    3. Machine gun tears up ground around him
    4. Flattens himself face down beside the dead man

Our protagonist now has more sensitive thoughts about the dead sniper. He has a strong compulsion to find out who the man is. In small but significant steps, he has grown in sensitivity all the way to the climax.

IX. "Then the sniper turned over the dead body and looked into his brother's face."[13]

The *climax* and *conclusion* are jelled in one sentence, but the conflict does not end there. The shock of a momentarily revived soul faces a tragic truth: He has killed his brother. The first requirement for a successful story has been met. The story is complete. Our protagonist is motivated to act the way he does by strong influences introduced internally and externally. The ironic turn at the end strongly emphasizes the theme: "War's destruction wears many faces, physical and psychological. Nobody wins."

The final requirement for fiction is also clearly developed—*inevitability*. Families are divided. Brother fights brother, and war eventually exacts its terrible price. When the end comes, conflict is stronger than ever, crowning the theme.

12

Themes: Underlying Ideas

The importance or necessity of story elements such as character, dialogue, viewpoint, and atmosphere are readily comprehensible. Students gain a genuine appreciation for these as they seriously ponder ways to present story materials effectively. But for many beginning writers, theme is ignored or pushed aside as an item of little consequence while they are engrossed in actually writing the story.[1]

Beginners fail to realize that the theme is the avenue through which you provide your ideas about life. Most writers agree these ideas serve as a supportive guide while plotting stories. Of course, we mustn't spell out the theme for our readers (though, at the moment of resolution, some of us feel strongly inclined to point out the truth we've implied in the story); instead, we should make these truths become evident in the thoughts and speeches of certain characters, never by narrative exposition. Always present your theme as subtly as possible.[2]

Theme Defined

The *theme* is the moral, the lesson, or the idea that grows in our minds when we look back upon the story. Some element, or a combination of elements, presents an idea that manifests itself beyond and above the happenings in the story. From explorations of human behavior, an author brings to light some facet of truth that may or may not be obvious to us and must be interpreted by us.

Themes from Escape Fiction

If the story depicts believable people in a highly controversial, emotional, or dramatic life situation, we can probably agree upon a statement of theme, the controlling central idea unifying the story. The writer has studied the prejudices and desires of his readers. His stories bring these prejudices and desires to the forefront, allowing them to please or anger us the way we expect escape stories to do. We know what to expect. Writers of these stories intend for us to enjoy each step of the story from beginning to end; they shock us with horror; they keep us in stitches with their humor; they make us search our windows and doors to make certain they are locked before getting back to that exciting murder thriller. We read and ask for more of the same. When readers pick up escape stories, they are not in the mood for forming statements about life.[3]

If the various escapades leave us with several ideas about life, the episodes might be set in a highly charged environment that is laced with symbols, allegorical passages or other elements, which readers must interpret. In such instances, the writer has woven a blend of escape and quality fiction. Escape fiction, however, is written entirely for pleasure, is predictable, and leaves little to be interpreted by the reader.

The theme may be used as a unifying feature of an escape story, but its content will then be universally appealing. The statements about life will be familiar ones, such as: "Don't count your chickens before they hatch"; "God don't love ugly"; or "Blood's thicker than water."

Actually, in story analysis, try to avoid using such platitudes. Even though they may accurately state a particular theme, relying upon them allows us to think less about additional themes that might be evident in the same story. The truth is, most themes may be expressed in several different ways. So, if your first impulse is to state your theme in some ready-made phrase, don't give in to it.[4]

Themes from Quality Fiction

If the theme is expressed through patterns of details, character, and symbols, uncovering it is more difficult. We find ourselves pondering an important image or some question about life. The answer to the question or the identification of the image becomes clear only when we are able to tie the descriptive details together to uncover a way of life, a behavior, or a vivid characterization. In these quality stories, much is left for the reader to interpret.

Only the details and symbols must be clear to readers in this instance; we weigh their significance in the light of our own experiences and agree or disagree with the statement the writer has presented for us. If the idea is wrapped in carefully selected details, we can gather these descriptive images and complete the shape of character and setting, conflict and theme. Only then do we see the truth our writer has painted. This truth is interpreted by readers who might be enlightened, saddened, amused, or upset by story events and what was implied in the writing. The theme is thus the author's view of any situation or question involving man and his relationship to man or nature. An exciting story will get us involved with the characters and the details, which are layered or blended to produce the desired effect.

Themes from Experience

Themes originate from experiences—the writer's and your own. Without experiences, the author would not be able to create the realistic situations that lead to his characters' credible decisions. There would be little information to provide for fresh understanding about people and their behaviors. In the same vein, without experiences, the reader would not be able to share the same understanding. He would not grasp all the implications the writer has skillfully woven into the plot.

Experience is the sound, the sight, the taste, the smell, and the touch of nature and humanity in day-by-day life situations. These perceptions are recorded deep within our brain where they quietly help us identify similar details in the world around us or in the world re-created within the pages of fiction and nonfiction.

We balk when characters and situations do not act according to the images and traits the author has drawn for us. At the same time, we are unable to grasp the theme of a poorly drawn story—one that does not provide the essential details for us clearly to delineate a moral or idea. The plot becomes an unconquerable maze of vague symbols and details that do not help us interpret human character.

What Comes First?

Every writer has to decide when to establish clearly his story's theme. The theme should be developing in the back of your mind as you begin constructing plot ideas, characters, and setting. You will first have a good idea for your story and where you want to take your protagonist. This character's image and much of his heart and soul are firmly implanted in your notes, as well as in your subconscious. Now you are ready to formulate your theme—that is, What do you want your story to say? Whatever your protagonist becomes, whatever he says, does, and thinks, and whatever goal he fixes on helps you establish the story's theme. The results should be a theme that is "neither too wide nor too narrow," but scaled to fit the story itself.[5]

Theme Found in the Title

Writers sometimes use their themes to title their stories. However, in many of these, the title expresses a platitude, and the reader reads on to discover a theme of deeper meaning. The effect is then similar to that of recognizing the significance of symbolic references made in the story when the symbol first appears in the title.

Henri Duvernois carefully selected his details and gave us a sharply defined character whose actions, though humorous and surprising, do fall within the bounds of credibility. Let's examine a brief synopsis of his story, "Clothes Make the Man" to help us uncover the theme:

Tango, considered to be lacking when it came to grey matter, was selected to become a watchdog for a caper his friends had plotted. They planned a heist, but they needed Tango somewhere close by to blow a whistle if there was any danger of someone discovering them. Tango was given a policeman's uniform, a badge, and a whistle. He dressed and studied himself in the mirror; from that moment until the climax, he began his transformation. In the street, he performed several worthy policeman's functions. By the time his friends had completed their scheme and were scaling the walls onto the street, Tango had been completely transformed. He blew his whistle, shouting, "Stop! I arrest you in the name of the law!"

The title is "Clothes Make the Man," and the theme—"Clothes make the man"—is a humorous statement about a lesson learned. To avoid the simplified platitude, however, let's phrase the theme with a more serious wording: "The best formed plans include knowledgeable, reliable men for carrying them out successfully."

Hawthorne: Sin and Its Effects

Nathaniel Hawthorne was concerned with the sins of the world and their effects upon human life. As an example of theme, let's consider his novel, *The House of Seven Gables.* The plot deals with the greed and power of Colonel Pincheon, who inflicts a great wrong against Matthew Maule. These two men are heads of their families, and the death of Maule begins a long reign of misfortunes for the Pincheons, resulting from the evil curses Maule had conjured upon them before he died. Leaders of each succeeding generation are inflicted with the curse, which does not end until Phoebe Maule and Holgrave Pincheon are married. The theme: "Man will reap the evil he sows."

Again, in his short story, "Dr. Heidegger's Experiment," Hawthorne is concerned with the sins of his characters, four aged men and a woman. First, there appears Doctor Heidegger, himself, who has loved and lost under strange circumstances. In the beginning, we are told that fifty-five years earlier he had prescribed a potion for his bride-to-be, and she had died. This past explains the appearance of the rose pressed within the pages of a book. As his "experiment" begins, he introduces the rose and displays the pitcher of water from the Fountain of Youth to the four aged friends who sit before him—three men and the widow Wycherly. He places the rose into the container of water, and it returns to its former beauty. The four are instantly moved and become interested in drinking the water of youth. The doctor suggests that they consider some rules to help them maintain a proper youth. They are eager to drink the water and become young again. They drink and, a short time later, are young again.

Dr. Heidegger's experiment is to answer the question, "If given an opportunity to become young again, will we return to our former sinful lives?" The four do return to the sins of their youth, and Hawthorne is suggesting that we would do the same. The characterizations, the foreshadowing, and the goals of the four provide us with our theme: "Man must change to keep what he has," or "If given an opportunity to live our lives over again, we will repeat the sins of our past."

Symbols that Parallel the Theme

Stephen Crane's *The Red Badge of Courage* explores the spiritual and psychological development of an eighteen-year-old Henry Fleming. He explores the youth's developing conscience and soul on the brink, in the midst, and after his first battle. Through our experience we witness how Henry develops in character as well.[6]

The battle is symbolic of the point in Henry's life when he feels the greatest pressure. This pressure brings about a significant change in Henry. The flag he carries forward in battle is his conscience. Conscience is further symbolized by the "cathedral forest" where the youth retreats to nurse his "guilt" wound. These and other symbols parallel the action and the theme and lend emphasis to the changes Henry must undergo to obtain his spiritual growth.[7]

When we review Henry's motives, his goals, and his actions, we are able to follow his transformation from the idealistic youth who holds a romantic view of war to the sharply contrasted young man who knows war as it really is. Henry gathers new insights from the long days of waiting, from the first blood drawn from the rebel cannons, and from the cathedral forest where a spiritual awakening opens his eyes to the truth. Pressure from the battle that finally takes place becomes the catalyst that opens Henry's conscience to this truth and, with his spiritual change, nourishes his transition into manhood.[8] The theme: "Man's salvation depends upon change and spiritual growth."

Propaganda Themes

Propaganda can be the all-intended purpose behind campaign slogans, television commentaries, speeches, plays, short stories, novels, and even nonfictional accounts. Propaganda is a powerful means of moving people to act the way you want them to act. The propagandist wants us to support a candidate, a government policy, a new idea, a political party, or a nation's war or peace efforts.

During World War II, Joseph Goebbels became Adolph Hitler's minister of propaganda. Goebbels glorified the nation's efforts even as the allied armed forces were closing a tight ring around Germany. His efforts drew the German people to the support of the cause, and factories turned out vast quantities of war materials.

Not all propaganda is as rampant with lies as were the speeches broadcasted to the Germans and their allies. Propaganda may only explore the facts, which, as presented, make a particular thing appear right or wrong, good or bad. Each piece of information may indeed be truthful. A work is propaganda, then, when any information contrary to the propagandist's purpose is deliberately suppressed. Of course, he never tells us he is presenting a one-sided report, for then we wouldn't be moved in the direction he wants.

The Jungle, a novel by Upton Sinclair, is an appeal to voters to take a new socialist movement to heart. The novel focuses upon the abuses to the stockyard workers and the unsanitary conditions of the meat packing industry. In addition, the author has uncovered the plight of immigrant laborers who, at that time, worked cheaply in the stockyards and the meat-processing plants around Chicago. Jurgis Rudkis, a powerfully built Lithuanian immigrant, is caught up in a cruel poverty trap within a system that does not allow him to break out.

Ironically, the novel became the springboard for new legislation aimed at improving the abominable sanitary conditions of this industry. The nation and its leaders were quick to rectify the wrong done to the place where the story hit hardest—their stomachs. Sinclair failed, however, to touch their hearts.[9] The theme: "Man's inhumanity to man must be identified and reckoned with."

Theme and Allegory

"Bartleby" is an *allegorical tale* whose two key figures are Bartleby, a scrivener, and a lawyer who gives Bartleby a job as a copyist for his firm. Upon careful examination of the plot and the characterizations of these two unususal people, you will probably agree that the lawyer becomes the protagonist. His concern for Bartleby, who is mentally ill, is a chronicle of frustration and of an uncommon concern for the welfare of someone who was only recently a stranger. As the plot unfolds, many subtle changes occur in the emotional development and in the behaviors of the main characters.

Questions you might ask yourself while reading this story include: Why did the lawyer continue to show concern long after he had fired Bartleby? How much does any of us owe someone who is a relative stranger? The lawyer continues to provide for Bartleby after the scrivener refuses to work and after the sick man is finally committed to an institution, intrigued by the fact that Bartleby refuses any help. Still, the only bond between the two men is a common humanity—one from which the lawyer cannot escape.[10]

The story ends with the lawyer paying a visit to the institution and discovering that the man is dead. He had refused the extra food the lawyer had provided. In spite of the fact that the lawyer had taken responsibility for the sick man, when he could do no more, he was left feeling miserable.

The theme is made clear to us through the events in the story. Remember, this is an allegorical tale, and what we feel about our responsibility toward strangers has much to do with our acceptance or rejection of the theme. But the theme is still there, giving us something to think about. The lawyer undergoes subtle changes as Bartleby's behavior becomes increasingly more difficult for him. In the process, he grows as a richly humane figure. When the scrivener dies in the institution, the lawyer is left feeling a deep loss. He gives us the theme himself in a verse from the Bible: "A new commandment give I unto you, that ye love one another." The story is thus concerned with man's love for man, simply because he's a man.

Themes that Shock Us

Shirley Jackson's story, "The Lottery," has been acclaimed as a chilling masterpiece. Students of prose fiction have studied its contents repeatedly to identify the author's purpose in writing it. Discussions have revolved around possible origins from the Old Testament, origins that help students find behavioral similarities for the horrible annual rituals performed in the small American farm communities; but identical parallels are lacking. Though Naboth, a Jezreelite, was stoned to death, he was killed because Ahab, the King, wanted the man's vineyard. This act was, undeniably, cruel and barbaric, but as shocking as it is, Ahab had a motive. "The Lottery," does not.[11]

"The Lottery" shocks us because of its senseless horror. We ask ourselves why the lottery continued to be held year after year. Wasn't there one man or woman willing to stand up and fight the custom? We recall several youngsters commenting about changes in other towns nearby, but these are scoffed at by Old Man Warner.

We ask, "Why did the author write this story?" Perhaps the horrible nightmare is meant as only a starting point, a place for us to take off in thought. Perhaps she wrote it to become a parable of modern times. Today, violence breaks out all the time, and we haven't any answers to it. Perhaps Shirley Jackson wanted us to examine outworn or destructive laws and customs and the directions these have taken us; perhaps we are being encouraged to turn from senseless behaviors and policies. How much reliance are we placing upon tradition? How many things are being done today simply because they were done that way before?[12]

Through examination and discussion of the details of a story, we can arrive at its theme. Let's recall a universal theme: "Man against man." Is that what everything eventually leads to here? If so, then we are able to say, "Man's inhumanity to man must be examined, questioned, and resisted with consummate vigor." Or, "Tradition must be examined and cleansed of man's inhumanity to man."

Uncovering the Theme

Now let's bring the importance of the theme into a clearer focus. We have seen that writers don't always write their stories with any theme in mind; some crime fiction, mysteries, adventure stories, and others are primarily plotted and written to entertain us with their excitement, suspense, and adventure. We delight in the tightly woven, fast moving plots that keep us reading toward that climax and resolution we are led to expect. Rarely do we look back and reassemble the details or stop to interpret anything that has happened.

Interpretation here is simply recognizing what is happening to our characters and to the forces opposing them, for these are escape stories, meant to take us away from our everyday problems. Most of us enjoy leaving normality behind for a moment of relaxation, reading stories about others who have erred, won and lost, or lost and regained. We enjoy stories that pull us into the ideal world of the romantics, into the amazing world of science fiction, into the mad world of horror and the occult, and into the imaginative worlds of fantasy and space. When we do uncover a theme in these stories, we recognize that it has been mechanically structured as a hook on which to attach the plot.

Then there are the stories that are built upon patterns of atmosphere, character, and symbols. The atmosphere often plants subtle, descriptive details that, when pulled together, help us complete a riddle or an idea that then opens the door to meaning and a fuller understanding of the story and the author's purpose. Perhaps there are symbols that must be interpreted to open every door and bring all elements of the pattern together. We are encouraged to think more about our discoveries, uncovering fresh ideas about life.

When we read these stories, we read with the understanding that we will need to draw upon our own knowledge of man and his world and upon our own personal experiences to interpret theme. We may not agree with the messages we find, but after evaluating them, we should be able to see the ideas presented in a clearer light.

The *quality story* always has a theme that must be interpreted from the details, actions, the character's spoken words, and from any symbolic references. Still, an author may provide a narrative passage or dialogue to help us understand the meaning or theme. Such passages are called "thematic passages." A brief thematic passage appears in "Bartleby" when the lawyer quotes a passage from the Bible's Old Testament: "A new commandment give I unto you, that ye love one another."

Finally, remember to look for a deeper, broader vision of themes. Steer clear of platitudes, even though they may state the themes correctly. Platitudes too often fail to express the theme fully, often stating only superficial or minor themes. If you are inclined to use a popular platitude to state a theme, stop and think some more.

13

Plotting Short Story Patterns

The sixth key element in fiction is the *plot,* a step-by-step organization of events. Some writers have favorite patterns for their plots; others use a different pattern each time they write a new story. Some don't pattern a story plot until they first make a thorough study of their principal characters; others insist upon working up an extensive plot before they develop characters suited to the action and the conflict. Then there are those gifted individuals who, with only a blank sheet of paper in the typewriter and hardly more than a few exciting ideas bouncing around in their heads, emerge with unforgettable characters, vivid scenes, and a plot marked by a remarkable blend of imagination and a unique ability to tell a good story.

No matter what method a writer uses to get his story down on paper, the end result provides us with useful patterns for study and application. We read and get the feel for each story and its action. We follow the plot sequence, the positioning of the story's key parts, the techniques of characterization, atmosphere, and revealing dialogues. We discover elements that are dominant and others that are missing or barely evident. Gradually, after reading dozens of stories, we begin to get a feel for the varying story patterns that offer us such a rich variety of writing styles, subjects, designs, lengths, and themes.

Three Story Structures

A short story may use one of three structural patterns: (1) the formula story, (2) the concealed plot, or (3) the no-plot pattern.

The Formula Story

Most *escape fiction* is patterned upon familiar plot segments, each having a distinct purpose in advancing the story to a satisfactory and exciting conclusion. The plot elements are obvious to readers who read often: (1) introduction, (2) minor crisis, (3) major crisis, (4) climax, and (5) denouement or conclusion.

The Concealed Plot

Many *quality stories* use this structure. This category will use one or two dominant elements to tell the story. Characterization and plot developments often depend upon the selective details uncovered in the setting, in the mood, and in the use of symbols. "The Japanese Quince," examined thoroughly in the next chapter, is an example of a story with a concealed frame. The six plot segments are there, but you have to interpret the descriptive details, the actions of the characters, and thoughts and dialogues to find them. *Implications* may also provide clues to concealed parts.

Simple, No-Plot Patterns

This simple pattern was popular in the 1940s, often appearing in the pages of *Redbook* and other popular magazines noted for their short fiction. Many short-short stories of one thousand to fifteen hundred words are woven around a single situation. Though the five major story segments do not appear, the structures retain whatever elements will produce a single effect, usually one charged with emotion. The pattern depends upon one key setting, with descriptive imagery and moods that immediately achieve reader identification with the thoughts and actions of the characters. The conclusion is usually dependent upon a little twist of irony that leaves the reader saying, "Yeah, that's what is really important," or "Yeah, that's the way it should be." We are sometimes surprised, but more often we are left with a good, gutsy feeling about people. Today there is evidence of a trend in the return of these no-plot patterns in popular magazines that use short fiction.

A Writer's Choice

Again, the *story's plot* is its frame or pattern. This frame contains the elements and techniques needed to get the results the writer wants. How the writer arranges the key parts of the story, laying them down in proportions that will draw and hold readers' interest, is often determined after much deliberation and, sometimes, after several revisions.

Some patterns place little emphasis on character but are constructed heavily around atmosphere and theme. Others depend heavily upon character and plot. The pattern may be experimental and, therefore, slightly confusing for the inexperienced reader but sophisticated readers of quality stories both expect and relish a challenge.

Key Parts of the Formula Pattern

In *modern escape stories,* the familiar plot pattern is woven around the five basic plot segments. In some plots, one or two of these segments are blended, however. More writers are beginning their stories with a minor crisis, what our protagonist thinks, says, and does serves as the introduction. The crisis mushrooms when the protagonist fails in his initial efforts, whereupon he is faced with a major crisis. Meanwhile, the actions and reactions, the characterizations, the setting, and the objectives of both protagonist and antagonist are revealed in small, sequential doses as the plot proceeds toward the climax. Each situation is carefully designed and measured, giving the information we need without stopping too long to explain what has happened or what will happen.

Transition through Exposition

Exposition paragraphs are essential, however, to keep the reader aware of transitions between scenes and to provide background information necessary for the next situation. Here, of course, we feel the presence of the narrator. Exposition, then, should be briefly interwoven into the action of the story, perhaps by using dialogues and the thoughts of characters.

Researching Your Facts

Whether you are writing fiction or nonfiction, accuracy in reporting factual information is essential. In science fiction, for example, if the story is set on the moon, the writer should research the moon's surface and atmosphere or lack of it. Readers might have to be apprised of the gravity differences between the moon and earth, or a number of other differences, such as the way a person would walk. Lack of air will govern the dress of individuals. And what about sound? Without air, there are no sounds other than those created within the space suit or from the system of communication attached to it. In science fiction, then, such differences can quickly complicate things for writers who fail to do their homework. On the other hand, facts can be used to generate the conflict your science fiction plots need.[1]

Some facts, however, may not be essential for telling your story. Mystery writers need not stop to describe a gun or to explain what fingerprints are. Authors of western novels and short stories do not have to provide detailed word-pictures of familiar objects, such as, horses, sheriffs, gamblers, and steers. And the authors of love stories know that the mores and customs of our society are too well-known to require a detailed explanation of every romantic mood or action.[2]

Isaac Asimov, a prolific science fiction novelist and author of many short stories in this category, tells us that science fiction requires explanations and descriptions of gadgetry and customs. What we often accept in the course of our lives may be radically different in such stories. We might not feel comfortable with what is taking place in these strange settings, under these circumstances, yet we are still interested in the unknown and the surprises it holds for us.[3]

Five Parts of the Formula Story

Here the five major short story segments, most of which are identifiable in escape fiction, are further defined:

I. The Introduction
   A. Introduces the principal character

B. Provides an appropriate atmosphere
C. Reveals a need or an aim of our protagonist
D. Plants the seed for conflict (may use a symbol to foreshadow trouble ahead or to parallel some other story element)

II. The Minor Crisis
A. Protagonist meets opposition or faces difficulties that threaten to deny him/her success or happiness (clashing goals)
B. Protagonist's effort to overcome the initial problem is foreshadowed
C. Protagonist is unsuccessful; problem looms larger; reader is concerned

III. The Major Crisis
A. Failure may expose a weakness
B. Protagonist attempts to correct mistakes or to try a stronger method to defeat or overcome opposition
C. Problem mushrooms when protagonist fails again
D. Protagonist draws upon resources to end the problem once and for all; fate and outside support must not do the job (although fate may certainly introduce new problems)
E. Foreshadowing of success planted earlier in the story now reveals a new strength of determination, a knowledge gained from his failing efforts, a talent or skill that has gone unnoticed

IV. The Climax
A. Marks the highest point in the rising action
B. Protagonist acts to resolve the conflict

C. Clues planted earlier make the next step inevitable and satisfying

V. The Conclusion

A. Story conflict is resolved in a win, lose, draw, or a win-suffer ending

B. Story leaves us with a better understanding of others and ourselves, or the story poses a question about life that we are left to interpret for ourselves

The Incident

Formula stories are usually written around three or four incidents or events, one or more of which the writer may deal with in a brief flashback, a character's thoughts, an expositional paragraph or two, or perhaps an interesting dialogue. One incident, however—the climax—must be drawn precisely from the actions of the principal characters, culminating from the other incidents. The length of this prose fiction genre makes brevity and precision essential.

An incident is a happening. The formula plot depends upon several kinds of incidents, planned for specific, but different, purposes:[4]

1. The *plot incident* is intended to move the plot another significant step toward its resolution.

2. A *character incident* is designed to reveal character. In Chapter 8, you learned several methods for developing character.

3. A *setting incident* occurs in a particular time and place to lend authenticity to the story and a feeling of "presence" for the readers.

4. The *symbolic incident* provides a parallel to an event in the plot or may emphasize character, setting, or theme. The symbolic incident found in "The Scarlet Ibis," to be discussed in Chapter 17, is the appearance of the great bird during a terrible storm. In that incident, the symbol's purpose is to foreshadow the climax, a plot incident.

5. The *obligatory incident* is included when the writer is obliged to supply information the reader needs because events are confusing or serious questions must be answered to maintain the credibility of characters, events, or of the writer.

Episodes

An *episode* is one segment of a novel's plot, but is generally the entire content of the short story. This segment includes all the incidents that comprise the protagonist's struggles to overcome opposition to his quest. In the short story when the episode ends, the story ends.

Novels, on the other hand, include several episodes, each developed more fully than the last. The novel's length affords an opportunity to explore every facet of an episode. Each episode may be interwoven skillfully with others, until all episodes are brought together prior to or during the climax, where all loose ends are resolved.

To understand exactly what can take place within the creative boundaries of an episode, we first need to recall a familiar plot, one that is easily accessible. Since a short story usually occurs completely within the bounds of one episode, let's examine a couple of episodes from a mainstream novel.

Some of us have seen the television adaptation of Herman Wouk's historical romance, *War and Remembrance,* and some have read it and followed the tragic tale of Aaron Jastrow's efforts to survive as a writer, a human being, and a Jew before and during the German occupation of Italy and France and ends with his death in a Nazi gas chamber. All those who tried to help him, who loved and admired him, and who envied and persecuted Aaron Jastrow are a part of the Jastrow–Nazi Holocaust episode. This episode is a significant part of the novel's frame, at various times affecting the lives of every principal character.

Some of the people who are drawn into this episode are actually structured in episodes of their own. Natalie, Aaron Jastrow's niece, and Byron Henry, a young, adventuresome American who is the son of an American naval officer and diplomat, are drawn together. Natalie is an important part of Aaron Jastrow's episode, and she becomes the romantic figure in Byron Henry's episode. The Byron Henry–Natalie Jastrow episode is probably a good working title for this segment. Fortunately, this one ends on a happier note when the two find their young son, who had been missing since the mad scramble prior to the German defeat.

There are other equally important episodes in this lengthy novel. Each gives us a look into a number of lives that span and shape an era, beginning with Pearl Harbor and ending soon after the atomic attack upon Japan.

Organizing Short Story Patterns

Studying the episodes of novels helps us understand how the episode of a short story differs. For one thing, the length of a short story does not allow as many incidents and, therefore, does not provide the greater story dimension needed for prolonged suspense. In effect, the short story is a more difficult, demanding writing experience and a skilled refinement of an author's storytelling ability.[5]

Edward D. Hoch, author of almost seven hundred short stories, encourages us to tantalize our readers at the start and to plot endings that leave them satisfied. Strong openings draw readers into the story, and a strong closing line adds another touch of magic. Readers are not only left feeling satisfied with the story, but they begin looking for other stories the author may have written.[6]

Hoch points to the opening sentence of Graham Greene's novel, *Brighton Rock*, published in 1938, as an example:

> Hale knew before he had been in Brighton three hours, that they meant to murder him.

Hoch considers this opening to be one of the best he has uncovered in the entire field of mystery and suspense fiction. The setting and the conflict are introduced in a brief sixteen words.[7] The ending is equally effective:

> She walked rapidly in the thin June sunlight towards the worst horror of them all.

Eventually, no matter how much the short story writer knows about his characters or their plights, he will organize his plot to produce a single effect, and he will revise and slant his stories anew to achieve it.

One consideration the writer must keep in mind, however, is the story's length. The current *Writer's Market* requirements may convince him to cut the original length from five thousand words to three thousand, a length popular with the magazines he's planning to contact.

Organizing the Formula Story

Here are the *organizational plans* available to a writer of conventional formula stories:

1. Begin the story at the beginning. The writer introduces the principal character and presents him/her with a problem. The character's reaction brings failure, or increased difficulties present themselves, and the hero/heroine is faced with a greater, almost unsolvable problem. This is the major crisis. We then follow the rapid rise to the climax. In the process, we get subtle and sharp descriptions of the character's strong, imaginative powers, inner strengths and convictions. Through his/her own efforts, a character draws upon these strengths and succeeds, leaving us with a better understanding of characterization and the need for planting strong and subtle traits that eventually decide a character's fate. The author has begun the story at the beginning and has carried us through a single episode, in chronological order. A troublesome conflict faced by the principal character has been assessed and acted upon in a fashion we find exciting and believable. We are often left with an understanding about one particular problem, and we may or may not be given a direct line to the story's theme. Most escape fiction leaves little doubt about the message the author intended. In quality fiction, the theme may be included or strongly hinted at in the title itself, however writers are apt to present characters, actions, and events that raise controversial questions, leaving the answers for us to decide. From both questions and answers, we are able to uncover the theme.

2. The author begins his story at a crucial moment prior to the climax and then takes us back in time. From this new beginning, he brings us up to the crucial moment a second

time. We see our hero or heroine overcome the problem, and the episode ends as the story ends.

3. The author devises a special formula of his own. One of these, used often in children's stories, is based upon incidents presented in threes. "The Three Little Pigs," find three little pigs building three different houses. The wolf enters the first two and begins his attack upon the third where all three pigs are holed up. Follow this with three unsuccessful efforts to get the owner out of the house, the final effort ending with the wolf's defeat.

4. The writer may begin at the beginning and use a couple of brief flashbacks, returning after each of these to the point where he left off.

Writers continue to experiment with organizational patterns that best present their stories. The beginning writer can become familiar with many such patterns by reading and analyzing stories in the quarterlies as well as those in commercial magazines.

14

Formula, Concealed Plot, and No-Plot Stories

Developing a Story Synopsis

Writers sometimes plan their stories thoroughly before they write them, drafting first an extended synopsis of the plot and then a fully developed outline. Such complete structuring of the story plot often exposes weaknesses that can be remedied before the piece is written. The writer may decide to insert a symbolic incident to enhance the theme. He may even replace a character incident with a more effective one. This planning process assures the writer that he will have a solid foundation for producing a single effect. The *synopsis* will not include every detail of an action or reaction, but it should certainly contain those details relevant to the story's key parts.

The best way to understand story structure is to develop and then study a synopsis. Let's use James Thurber's "The Catbird Seat" as an example.

Here we have a humorous escape story. Thurber presents us with clear-cut characterizations of our protagonist and antagonist, and there is little left, beyond supportive implications, for the student to interpret. Note how Thurber's story pattern aligns with the key story segments. At the same time, we can observe the distinct organizational pattern as well. Does the story begin at the beginning and follow through in chronological order to the end?

Introduction:

Mr. Martin, an efficient filing clerk for F & S, plots a murder. Mrs. Ulgine Barrows has been with the company for several weeks, and our clerk has decided to "rub her out." On his way to her apartment, he stops at a small shop for some cigarettes, though he is known at the office as a nonsmoker and a teetotaler.

Minor Crisis:

His perfection as a key filing clerk had gone uncontested before Mr. Fitweiler appointed the woman as his special adviser. That's when several employees were fired or left on their own accord. The woman put her nose into every office, making life miserable for everyone. Mr. Martin, a quiet man who took great pride in his filing system, decided he had to act quickly before she caused him to lose the job he enjoyed.

Major Crisis:

He pays a visit to her apartment and searches for a weapon to do her in. Nothing appears right for the job. She offers him a drink. He accepts. He smokes a few cigarettes, much to the woman's dismay. Then he gets the idea of presenting himself as a drug addict, a heavy smoker, and all the terrible things he isn't, although she doesn't know this. When he explains how he plans to make a bomb and blow Mr. Fitweiler to smithereens, she orders him out of the house.

Climax:

The next morning, Mrs. Barrows does exactly as he had hoped she would do. She announces that she is going to tell Mr. Fitweiler all about the abominable man who came to her apartment with his horrible plot. The president eventually asks Mr. Martin about it. He denies it. Mrs. Barrows breaks into the office, hysterically protesting his guilt.

Mr. Martin remains calm and innocent. Mr. Fitweiler, having a high regard for Mr. Martin's total abstinence from liquor and tobacco, decides that the woman is suffering from a persecution complex and orders his assistants to take her to her apartment.

Resolution:

Mr. Fitweiler apologizes to Mr. Martin for the embarrassment the woman caused. The clerk returns to his small cubicle, feeling the return to normalcy—a return to his "catbird seat."

Organization

The third person narrative begins with Mr. Martin buying a pack of Camels at Schrafft's on Fifth Avenue. The man recalls that the antagonist, Mrs. Barrows, has been with them a week. He is thinking of the perfect plot to murder Mrs. Barrows. Thurber's expositional paragraphs then bring in the facts behind her appointment as special adviser to the president of F & S. He tells us how she caused several employees to lose their jobs and has annoyed Mr. Martin on several occasions with her nosy inquiries and curious innuendoes. We then return to where we left Mr. Martin at Schrafft's on Fifth Avenue, and the plot moves forward again. Our protagonist purchases a pack of cigarettes and proceeds to the woman's apartment to complete his murder scheme. Except for the brief expositional passages telling of Mrs. Barrow's earlier disruptions in the office and of the facts behind her employment, the story moves forward in chronological order.

The Martin-Barrows episode includes a plot incident—when Mr. Martin plans to murder the woman. Character incidents are covered in expositional paragraphs where we are made to understand what Mrs. Barrows has been doing, and how she got her job (she charmed the boss with her concern for him).

We are given a character-plot incident in the woman's apartment. Here we get a taste of Thurber's humor. Mr. Martin's cunning strategy hints at an interesting ending, structured around three brief incidents: (1) a character-plot incident where Mrs. Barrows announces that she will tell all to Fitweiler; (2) a character-plot incident with Mr. Martin and Mr. Fitweiler discussing the issue; and (3) a resolving plot incident where the woman is declared emotionally unstable and driven to her apartment. A final scene allows us a brief glimpse of Mr. Martin quietly reclaiming the catbird seat.

Implications

Implications are implied feelings, deeds, motives, and reactions that can be uncovered in the setting, in characterizations, in conflict, in the theme, and in the plot. You will want to search stories for evidence to support implications you draw from the story. You might note the evidence and list the implications that can be drawn from it.

Example: How does Mr. Martin picture himself?
Answer: Mr. Martin considers himself to be efficient and worthy of his position. He is determined to maintain his outward dignity and his proven system of filing.
Evidence: His actions and thoughts reveal all.

Example: How does Mrs. Barrows see Mr. Martin?
Answer: She sees him as a weak, mousy, odd little man of questionable character.
Evidence: Her words to Mr. Martin and Mr. Fitweiler reveal her attitude. The implications are further supported by her plans to have his filing procedures investigated.

Identification

Writers make every effort to have us identify with specific characters. We may not like everything we learn about them, but we are able to support their determination to overcome human frailties and to use their talents or strengths to overcome oppression or certain disasters. We find ourselves pulling for the hero or heroine. We are hooked by character and events in a plot that makes us laugh or cry.

In "The Catbird Seat," Mrs. Barrows is the sort of person most of us consider to be annoying. Although Mr. Martin is meek in appearance, he is a man determined to keep his position and is envied for his cunning mind and the successful strategy he uses to thwart the woman's plans to have him dismissed. He is the character with whom most of us identify.

The Theme

As you review the synopsis and the segments of "The Catbird Seat," you will uncover the theme. Read over the following themes and decide which is more fitting for the story:

1. There are several ways for a man to end a problem.
2. The weak win out in the long run.
3. Appearances are deceiving.
4. Every man has a limit to what he will take.

While there may be some truth in the first and fourth themes, it is the third statement that comes closest to presenting the key, underlying idea.[1]

A Quality Story—Plot Often Concealed

The *quality story* will rarely please the readers of escape fiction, who demand lots of "blood and guts" action and a predictable ending. Some commercial magazines do publish interpretive, quality fiction, but most do not, for apparently more readers enjoy stories where very little needs to be intrepreted.

"Quality fiction poses questions and illuminates some aspect of human behaviors."[2] The reader interprets meaning for the characterizations, the plot, the tone, and the story's subject matter. Rarely do these stories have predictable endings. The patterns and treatment do not follow any formula, as escape literature does. Instead, the quality story takes us into the midst of life, removing veils of illusion and helping us see the shapes and forms of things; the writer's intent is to help us see, feel, and understand better.[3]

The summary of our quality fiction selection is expanded to include details pertinent to understanding the story pattern and the dominant elements. Here, too, a symbolic element illustrates how symbols can be very effective, as will be more fully explained in the next chapter. The selection is John Galsworthy's story, "The Japanese Quince."

Introduction:

Atmosphere and character are dominant elements at the beginning. As Mr. Nilson opens the window of his dressing room, we are given several descriptive details: Mr. Nilson is well-known in the city; he experiences a sweetish sensation in the back of his throat and a feeling of emptiness under his left rib. As he closes the window, he notices a small tree blooming in the garden. A check of the thermometer reveals a room temperature of sixty. Spring has come. His thoughts turn to the prices of Tintos* and quickly to a concern for his appearance. A glance into an ivory-backed handglass leaves him reassured. He puts on his black frock coat and goes downstairs.

In the dining room, his morning paper has been placed on a sideboard. He picks it up and again becomes aware of that queer feeling in his chest.

He opens the door and descends scrolled iron steps into the garden.

---

*Tintos (obsolete): The tint of a dye or wine (Oxford English Dictionary, p. 59, vol. 11, reprinted 1961)

The clock strikes eight. Breakfast is at eight-thirty. He has time for a turn in the gardens.

Mr. Nilson now paces a circular path, his morning paper clasped behind him. He notices that the feeling of emptiness is still there and that it is worse. He tries deep breathing, but it doesn't help. It is as though some "sweetish liquor" coursed through his body, "together with a faint aching just above his heart." He doesn't recall having eaten anything unusual the night before. Finally, he considers that the scent of spring blossoms might be the culprit, whereupon he moves closer to the tree to observe it more closely. Descriptions of the tree and its blossoms tell us that it is beautiful but unfruitful.

The Crisis:

Descriptive setting, action, and mood continue to be the pattern from which characterizations unfold.

Mr. Nilson's neighbor, Mr. Tandram, appears in the garden. The blackbird flies away. The two men find it difficult to converse and are able to speak only when they are discussing the bird or the tree. The tree has a tag identifying it as the Japanese quince. The conversation doesn't develop very far.

Major Crisis:

Atmosphere now reveals a number of details reflecting similarities in their walk, in each man clasping a newspaper behind his back. More importantly, the unsettling similarities the two men recognize in each other make the encounter in the garden too painful and too embarrassing for either man to continue a dialogue.

Climax:

Mr. Nilson and Mr. Tandram head back to their apartments; however, we learn that Mr. Nilson sees Mr. Tandram at his window, gazing out upon him and the garden. He hears the man cough and clear his throat as he, himself, has coughed so often. He sees the same scrolled iron steps leading to the rear entrance of each of the dwellings.

Finally, we learn that the blackbird has returned to the quince and is chanting out his heart in song.

Conclusion:

Mr. Nilson, feeling upset and unable to say why, enters his apartment and opens his morning paper.

Critique of the Story

The author takes us beneath the surface of the story with details and incidents that provide illuminating descriptions of two characters, Mr. Tandram and Mr. Nilson. They are identical in appearance and their predictable English behaviors. Their dull, sedentary lives follow habitual daily routines behind the walls of similar apartments with the same scrolled iron steps leading into the garden. These details tell us much about the characters. We follow their moves, collecting a sense of the customary English reserve when they face each other in the garden. No single detail does the entire job for us, but when the evidence is carefully assembled, we can see into the characters and the lives they live.

This is a quality story. The plot is based upon a pattern of characterizations, comparisons, recognition, and implications, using descriptive clues to help us identify concealed plot elements. Carefully selected details do what lengthy situations would not do: They give us a shorter, more compact story that is quite revealing of these men, the time, and the place.

The Symbol

In the garden, we are introduced to a symbol—the Japanese quince. The *symbol* must be interpreted to get the underlying idea: The quince produces only flowers—no fruit. There are no children. The two characters move in established, sterile routine that ignores the waves of progress, clinging adamantly to the status quo. This attitude was common for the turn-of-the-century middle classes Galsworthy depicts. Eventually, they get a glimpse of themselves, seeing each other for the first time. From that moment of recognition we discover the true antagonists: their stifling English reserve, their tiresome daily routines, and their sedentary habits. Each man recognizes himself in the other and turns away to avoid further embarrassment.

The ending must also be interpreted. Each man is disturbed by his discovery of himself in his neighbor, but neither man is amenable to change. The characters thus become symbolic of the property and merchant classes' resistance to change.

Conflict

The conflict arises from their own attention and devotion to the traditional values and customs of their business or merchants classes. Mr. Nilson suffers from circulatory and digestive problems he can't identify, and there are equally strong implications that Mr. Tandram is ill as well. Again, we are reminded of the truth each man has recognized about himself, as he witnesses it in the lifestyle and attitude of the other. Their ills will not disappear. The truth holds excitement for a moment, but it is less painful to ignore it, to return to apathy.

What's in a Name?

Laurence Perrine, author of *Literature: Structure, Sound, and Sense,* raises several questions concerning the names of the two characters in "The Japanese Quince." Has John Galsworthy consciously chosen these names because of the meanings they have? Perrine suggests that the name Nilson can be analyzed as "Nil's son—son of Nil or nothing," and the name Tandram comes from dram, a very small measure, and tan, a substance used for tanning hides to make leather.[4] What does this tell us? Perhaps the author used these names to emphasize the class rigidity and petty concerns of these English gentlemen.

The Author's Purpose

Galsworthy was influenced by the social and technological ills of the early 1900s. "Quality," another of his short stories, illuminates the author's deep concern for those caught up in the waves of modernization and social change, unable to cope with them or maybe unwilling even to try. In his novels, Galsworthy also criticizes the selfishness of the English property class, depicting them as being more interested in property than in human values.[5]

The "No-Plot" Pattern

"No-Plot" is a term used by some story analysts to describe the patterns of many short-short stories; however, even these very compact stories include plot segments in their patterns: (1) a setting and a character or characters that reflect upon earlier or current actions or interactions, either of these raising some question of truth, doubt, or perhaps hope; (2) a conclusion that brings truth to light, erases the doubt, or brings hope to fulfillment. The writer's magic comes through with a critical twist of irony, a twist that has been foreshadowed or made credible by carefully selected details in the situation.

Fiction elements are essential in all stories, some elements being more dominant than others. In the short-short, atmosphere provides a current of emotion; character emerges from descriptions of the setting and from the thoughts and actions of characters. Viewpoint and theme are present. If conflict is not a major element, the concluding portion will provide a significant turn of events, leaving us with a definite statement or feeling about others, ourselves, or about life in general.

About Writing Short Stories

Writing short stories, like all good writing, is demanding, certainly, but the process should be fun. Even when it flows effortlessly, the writer takes pains, consciously or unconsciously, to produce an interesting story.[6] Of course, a short story should not confine us to the exhausting labor the novel so often requires. Still, novels ought to be fun, too, and they often are, though they do include moments that are difficult to resolve, and therefore, become laborious and not as enjoyable.[7]

Writers write; all others procrastinate or talk about writing. If you're a writer, you're keeping a journal of the events and happenings around you that will eventually supply you with hundreds of ideas for stories to write and sell. Somewhere in the paths you take from day to day, something or someone will catch your interest: an unusual character, a unique setting, a moment you shared with a friend you haven't seen for years or with a complete stranger who held your fascination for a brief moment—any of these can hold the germ for a story. What observations did you make while visiting the shopping mall? the book stores? the ice-cream parlor? the doctor's office? Don't forget to record your feelings about anything or toward anyone. You can use these many experiences in your writing, and your readers will feel their authenticity. All details are relevant for writers. When you need a unique character, a situation, a scenic or familiar setting, they might be waiting in your journal.

15

Patterns for the Novel

How a writer structures a novel is a personal decision, one rarely made at the start. As your planning uncovers exciting opportunities for expansion, you may discover the need for a subplot. Additional characters may be needed to tell the story. Perhaps you began the story in the first person, and you now realize additional viewpoints necessitate the use of a third person, omniscient point-of-view. Other unexpected developments may encourage more changes. The category of story you plan to write will almost certainly have a lot to do with your novel's pattern possibilities.

Here are several patterns novelists use today:[1]

1. chronological order

2. use of subplots

3. ending first

4. diaries

5. letters

6. experimental patterns
   a. streams-of-consciousness
   b. counterpoint treatment

Chronological Order

When episodes are written in a sequential order, the pattern is known as *chronological order,* the most popular pattern among mystery writers and their readers. The protagonist becomes involved immediately in some sort of crime or mystery. One person usually tells the story from within the events or from the sidelines as a third person, limited omniscient reporter. Each episode may have its own crisis, followed by other episodes, until the climax is reached. Loose ends are then brought together to complete the whole and to leave the reader feeling satisfied. Readers remember each episode and can uncover the writer's pattern for telling the story.

The Murder Mystery

A sample murder mystery can serve to illuminate this patterning. Suppose the first episode covers the discovery of the body and the fear this discovery creates for the protagonist. He doesn't want to get involved with the police; however, the police arrive just as he has foolishly picked up a .38, his own, and he's standing there in the middle of the murder scene with the murder weapon in his hand. The police refuse to accept his explanation for his presence at the scene. He's taken to headquarters and held in custody until he can be fully interrogated.

Most mystery writers use a third person, limited omniscient viewpoint, entering the mind of only one character who will be in each scene of every episode. In this category, you also notice that each episode follows another, providing a tightly unified novel and a category formula for an escape fiction pattern that is easily recognizable.

Let's go back to the plot. The conflict grows as the protagonist finds himself being held for interrogation. The conflict introduced here helps you plot the next situation. You have to plan an escape, for your protagonist has very valid reasons for keeping a low profile. You'll invent some intriguing situation he's involved in—he's an undercover agent of some kind and doesn't want this fact discovered.

Of course, you'll have to decide what connection his undercover work has with the victim, how his own revolver ends up on the floor beside the dead man, and how he will convince the police that he's innocent. In any case, you have created additional conflict in his fear of discovery. Continually ask yourself questions, and the right answers will keep your mystery alive and moving.

What then? A real crisis: The agent is accused of the crime. Here is our first episode: the agent's-discovery-arrest-escape-accused episode. The next episodes follow end to end, with one episode dealing with his own undercover schemes, including a possible link with some previous scandal, and the continuation of his efforts to prove his innocence. With more questions and answers, you will connect the two episodes and create new ones, uncovering evidence that the dead man was connected with the agent's undercover investigation, and exposing government officials in a drug deal or an assassination attempt. The reader learns just enough information to keep him in suspense, learning it as soon as the agent does.

Other episodes present themselves as the novel broadens and deepens, but these two will run the length of your story. It is important that one episode be your main thread holding the plot in a tightly knitted, chronological pattern. The reader feels the agent's insecurity as an accused man being hunted down by the police. He feels the suspense of those undercover schemes involving our protagonist and begins to identify with his determination, his skills in search and detection. Finally, the reader is delighted with the unraveling of interesting details connecting the two episodes.

If there are additional episodes, each must be relevant to these two, and they should heighten the tension while maintaining a satisfactory pace.

Structuring Episodes

Robert Louis Stevenson's classic adventure, *Treasure Island,* follows a chronological pattern. One episode follows another until the very end.[2] Another example is Mark Twain's *Huckleberry Finn,* where we follow Huck from one series of incidents (an episode) to another. Note, however, that Huck's adventures involve him in episodes that do not depend entirely upon the events occurring in an earlier episode. Any number of incidents could have been used to replace others, as long as these maintained the atmosphere and conflict suitable for a boy whose principal objective is to help the slave, Jim, reach the river port of a free state. On the other hand, Mark Twain could have chosen episodes whose contents were dependent upon each other, making a link that could not have been broken without damaging the story. In such cases, each episode grows out of what happens in the previous one.

Revision in one episode may require drastic revisions in the next, and so on.

Subplots

Lengthy, complex novels require *subplots,* for instance, *War and Remembrance,* Herman Wouk's two-volume novel discussed in Chapter 13. The several episodes cited then are actually parts of subplots. One plot includes all the episodic events regarding Aaron Jastrow and his niece, Natalie. These would include Natalie's two loves and her travels to European cities to secure help for herself and her aging uncle Jastrow. It includes all the suffering imposed upon the Jastrows during their escape efforts, and their failure to stop the holocaust of human suffering and murder in the gas chambers, where Aaron Jastrow, himself, comes to a horrible end.

We must also consider Natalie's trip to America as part of the subplot. Her relationship with Byron Henry is just one of several episodes in her life. It converges the Jastrow-German subplot with the Pug Henry plot. Pug Henry is the anchor for the episodes involving American diplomacy in Europe prior to our entry into the war, his efforts to keep his flighty, promiscuous wife happy, his attempts to get to know his son, Byron, and the part he played in the war against Japan. The Byron Henry–Natalie Jastrow episode is the link used repeatedly to unify the whole by bringing the two subplots together in a series of conflicts affecting both segments.

Ending First

In our discussions of short story patterns, you learned that the ending-first pattern is sometimes used. For example, the novel might open with the condemned man going to the electric chair, the priest praying with the man, providing just the right moment to slip easily into a flashback to an earlier time, to the beginning. The writer then moves the story forward chronologically until we reach the point where we left the condemned man with the priest. Of course, the flashback may have uncovered information that now moves somebody to free the condemned man. Any ending will work that is true to character and presents reader satisfaction.

Diaries

John Hersey's *The Wall* is written as a diary of heroic deeds and suffering among Jews confined behind the walls of their Warsaw ghetto. There are a number of factual, published accounts of German atrocities carried out on these people during World War II. Today, novels of that period are again proving to be successful mainstream efforts that reach the top of the best-seller lists.

Probably the most successful diary ever published was a factual account by a Jewish teenager, Anne Frank. The girl's account, published after her death in a notorious Nazi internment camp, gives us an historic record of a family's suffering and humiliation under Nazi tyranny.

When American forces landed on Guadalcanal, one of the Solomon Islands in the South Pacific, Richard Tregaskis was there to write *Guadalcanal Diary*, an exciting account of the tenacity and heroism of Americans whose recapture of the island became a turning point in our war in the Pacific. In fact and in fiction, the diary format gives an effect of authenticity.

Letters

Several novels have been quite successful as fiction told

in a collection of *letters*. One of the oldest efforts at using this form was made by Samuel Richardson, an English printer, at the age of fifty-one. He may have been the first to use the form in his two-volume novel, *Pamela,* the first volume published in 1740.

Experimental Pattern: Streams-of-Consciousness

During the first half of the twentieth century, three English writers, Virginia Woolf, Katherine Mansfield, and James Joyce, produced novels and/or short stories in the experimental, *streams-of-consciousness patterns*. These stories carry us along with a series of long, descriptive passages, often interrupted with abrupt digressions stemming from a narrator's thoughts and feelings. These digressions might cover seconds, minutes, hours, or even longer periods of time. Sometimes the protagonist takes us in a grand sweep, gathering varied impressions of people, nature, and action and sharing a multitude of emotional reactions to them. At other times, we are able to follow fragmented images of changing light and shade, of excitement and boredom, of tension and release. Each sharply drawn descriptive statement flows easily, but might abruptly digress in other directions.

Virginia Woolf's Diary

Virginia Woolf began a diary in 1915 and continued to make entries until just a few days before her tragic death in 1941. Readers of her diary uncover her genuine passion for writing and rewriting until each sentence held images drawn to perfection. She was a severe critic of her own work; yet, she was highly sensitive to criticism from others. The extensive writings in her diary were carefully examined by her husband, Leonard Woolf, who selected those he thought had the most interest and lasting value and published them as *A Writer's Diary*.[3]

Developing a Streams-of-Consciousness Pattern

How does a writer develop a streams-of-consciousness pattern? One way is to turn to a setting and an event in progress from which we see the scene come alive. Build your scene in steps that reveal images, directions, thoughts, digressions, flashbacks, and elaborations. Then bring the reader back to center stage, to that point from which all other elements grew.

1. Suppose your setting provides the following initial images: a main street in a small town

winter and snow
a father buying boots for his son, David
a Christmas parade in progress
an army band playing holiday songs
an ambulance siren wailing from the parade line
an old war veteran, waving a tiny American flag

2. Choose your viewpoint character. For our purposes, let's stick with the father who is selecting a pair of boots for his son, David.

3. With the initial images planted firmly in your mind, close your eyes, letting your conscious spirit generate ideas that expand upon the starter images. Describe the sounds;

draw our attention to the people, to something about them that annoys, surprises, encourages, delights, or excites your protagonist. From any of these emotional experiences, one can easily take off in multiple directions.

4. Now bring us back to the key point or center stage again. Your eyes have become our eyes; your feelings are shared by us; or perhaps you have provoked a feeling of antagonism—no matter—your protagonist is on center stage again, and we sense a change in the attitude he displayed in the beginning.

> Before I open the door to Jeremy's and hear the bells tinkling, I realize I am making a mistake and nearly turn around to go back to my car. I wish now that I had, but my son, David wants boots—red leather boots, engraved with his name beneath a yellow rose—and here I am at Jeremy's where the salesmen act like they don't care whether you buy or not. It's Christmas, too, and the traffic's blocked out to leave the way open for the parade. Besides, my sinuses are acting up—always give me trouble in damp weather—and Jeremy's is as warm as toast inside their ritzy facade.
>
> Not a clerk in sight, but a minute later I bump into one in the shoe department—a thin, spectacled little man who looks more like a lifeless, dried-out mannequin in a window display. But this one moved.
>
> "May I help you, sir?" The voice might have come from a stuffed toy—the kind where you pull the string and the words spill out.
>
> "Boots for my son, David."
>
> "Anything special in mind?"
>
> "Boots for my son. He's twelve. Size eight." At least, I think that's the kid's shoe size. Will it be the same for boots?

Then the mannequin points a long thin finger in another direction. I look and there are boots racked in several rows, but the sign suspended overhead reads that this is the adult shoe department. No discount.

I hear the sirens wailing from the street. I know I should have gone over to Winchester—not much out of the way—for the prices are usually less. The sales people are nice too. Greet you with a smile and ask how the wife and kids are. I say, fine, thank you. How are you and your family?

"Just shop around," the mannequin says, his finger still pointing to the adult shoe department. "The prices are clearly marked."

An ambulance siren wails. I wonder if some child is hurt. They drive you nuts at Christmas. They want everything: fire trucks, tanks, guns, mechanical cars and trucks, rockets and launching pads—you nearly go mad for two days. Then you wise up, sneaking the stuff off to the incinerator to burn it.

"They come to see Santa," a woman said. She is very old. Her hair is the purest white.

A pert young sales lady pins the woman's purchase—a corsage of red and silver bells and a sprig of green holly—onto her coat's lapel. She moves toward the front of the store to stand at the huge glass window and watches the children outside.

It's snowing. I hate snow. Not when I was a kid, tracking it in and out. But I am drawn to the sounds of the marching band and the Christmas songs. And kids everywhere. Walking. Running. None are standing still.

Then I see his face, just outside the entrance. He presses it close against the glass door and looks in. The lines are old and weathered. Ninety, maybe. Tattered, brown army coat. He's a veteran of the Great War, I decide. He offers a wide, toothless grin. Now he steps back and waves a small American flag, left and right in front of him. A tear swells and breaks from the corner of his left eye. I turn away and cough to clear my throat.

"Did you find what you want?" the clerk asks. "I can help, if you like."

"No hurry," I tell him. "The parade . . . let's watch the parade."

Critique

Every detail reported to us through our first person narrator in this rambling streams-of-consciousness incident let's us know a little more about him. His thoughts, too, reveal a great deal more. Implications clearly define a character who enters Jeremy's against his better judgment (or so he thinks). Remember the earlier examples of writing with negative or positive emotion? One traveler painted the restaurant scene with gloom, for he was hurting inside; then there was the traveler whose heart was thrilled with the spirit of love at Christmas—he was able to share this feeling with others inside the restaurant. David's emotion changes when the actions of other customers, who express inner joys and compassion for the holiday season, have a powerful effect upon him. David is very real to us.

Counterpoint

Novels patterned upon *counterpoint* throughout introduce several apparently unrelated characters in separate themes, somewhat like one would find in a musical composition. They develop one character, then, follow another as the episodes are combined or continued in a parallel but contrasting action, giving the plot moments of conflict or harmony. The final effect is chaotic and difficult for many readers to follow. Sophisticated readers, those trained to understand such plots and themes, are able to separate the parts and keep tab of developments. Aldous Huxley's *Point-Counter-Point* is an example of this plot pattern.

Counterpoint plays a vital part in weaving contrast and conflict within small portions of the plot. For instance, a dialogue in counterpoint might involve people speaking and interrupting, listening to and ignoring what others do and say at an election eve party. But when the plot is framed entirely with characters and events laid out in counterpoint, the result can be disastrous for both the uninitiated and professional alike.

Novel Divisions

Novels aren't always divided into chapters; many have other parts or segments. Here are the more popular divisions found in novels:

1. Chapters.
2. Sections or segments, numbered more often in Arabic numerals but sometimes in Roman numerals. These numbered sections may go as high as one hundred or more.
3. Two or more parts, each including chapters or numbered sections. The chapters or sections are numbered consecutively from the beginning to the end of each part, or consecutively from the beginning to the end of the book, regardless of the number of parts. These parts may or may not have titles:

Part I The President is Missing
Part II Assignment in Lisbon
Part III Shadowing the Wolf
Part IV Springing the Trap

4. Unnumbered sections with two to four spaces between scenes. An example of this division is *The Sibyl,* the novel by Par Langervist, Swedish author, awarded the Nobel Prize for Literature in 1951.

5. Diaries and letters, each entry or letter dated for time order.

6. Some single volumes are divided into two or more books.

7. Some novels have two or more volumes: *Shogun, War and Remembrance.*

As you can see, your choices for your novel division are plentiful. You may even develop a new form, for no limits are imposed upon your freedom of imagination and talent for shaping your story and telling it the way you choose. Nevertheless, the final product must be published, promoted, purchased, read, and enjoyed before it can be considered a genuine success.

16

Constructing Unified Novel Patterns

Some novels are thinly and loosely drawn, whereas others are woven tightly, with depth and breadth of plotting and action paced appropriately. Books are woven into a tight finish through the use of a number of preplanned plotting and writing techniques, although some writers succeed through trial and error steps that eventually bring their novels to completion. If you've never tried your hand at writing a novel, however, much disappointment can be avoided by having a specific writing plan.

The following steps should prove helpful in preventing false starts and wasted hours of writing a first novel that ends up out of sync, out of psyche, and very likely destined for failure:

1. pre-thinking
2. developing character and situation data

3. drafting a rough outline
4. adding new material: characters, settings, events
5. selecting a point-of-view
6. selecting a unifying pattern
7. picking an exciting first incident
8. rethinking your outline
9. writing a rough draft
10. revising as often as necessary

Pre-thinking

First, you have to decide what type of novel you want to write. What kind of novels do you enjoy reading? Reading, dissecting, and analyzing books in the genre and category you enjoy reading most should encourage you to write the same kind of book. You're going to need a lot of excitement to carry you through the long haul of a novel.

Write about people and places with whom you can readily identify. If you've lived most of your life in a small town, naturally you know more about the people who live and sin there. Of course, with a little research you could eventually take us to New York, Hollywood, or to Paris, but you'll probably fare better with your first novel by writing about familiar settings and people.

Let's say you've chosen to write a mainstream novel set principally in rural Mississippi or Georgia. Your story is to become a vivid example of realism. Ask yourself these questions: Will the novel involve current or past historical incidents? Which of the many topical issues will it examine:

incest, rape, murder, wife beating, child abuse, or some other issue prominent in the news today? All of these, and more, are fertile ground for the mainstream novel. It is important to ask such questions before you begin writing the book. You need the answers early to begin selecting the characters and events that will bring the story to life.

Developing Characters and Situations

Although characters will grow as the plot unfolds, you can't begin writing your novel until you know the principal characters. Suppose you've chosen to write about the plight of textile workers in the South, for you've uncovered tragic tales of yellow lung disease, tuberculosis, and other infirmities associated with years of working in the cotton mills. What tragedies and conflicts might emerge for your protagonist in such a rural setting? In the small, cotton mill towns, earthy entanglements involving men and women who party, drink, and fight, especially on weekends when the mills are idle, are well-known. Other details reflecting their true natures might be uncovered by researching their rich heritage of patriotism for state and country or by investigating their strong family ties, especially in the face of adversity. Some of your incidents can illustrate this nature, and the plights of your protagonist will begin to take shape.

Your antagonists should be equally strong. The plant supervisors, the county sheriff or local constable, the merchants, the families who live in the shotgun mill houses, car salesmen, ministers, priests, or others who could serve as antagonists or minor characters will emerge as they are needed. You'll undoubtedly think of hundreds of situations that can occur, each offering characteristics to the protagonist and antagonist who will bring the story to life. But you will not use all of these situations, for pacing your novel with a careful selection of purposeful events, each patterned to increase the conflict and lead us on to an exciting conclusion, is the main idea.

When you've found your main thread, stick to it, letting the plot unravel in your head. When you have several good ideas for incidents, begin to establish a time element. When does the story take place? How much time will elapse from beginning to end? Make a note of these time elements. Now you are ready to begin a rough outline.

Drafting a Rough Outline

Drafting a rough outline should leave you with definite plans for a strong beginning, key situations for the middle, and an exciting ending. You might even plot the ending entirely and write a rough draft of the final chapter before going back to write the beginning. Once you have an exciting finish, you might find it easier to plot the events leading up to that point. Make sure to include action that provides increased tension and reader identification from beginning to end.

Choose how you will divide the sections of your book. For example, a novel of four hundred pages will produce a book of about one hundred thousand words. You might break this whole into twenty-five chapters of sixteen pages each. Purchase twenty-five nine-by-twelve manila envelopes, one for each chapter, and on the fronts and backs outline what is put inside.

Continue adding ideas and entire incidents for any part of the book, and place these in the appropriate envelopes. Some writers actually write complete first drafts of each incident before placing them in the chapter envelopes. Once you understand what plotting is all about, you'll work out your own strategies; however, don't forget to note any deletions or additions on the outside of the envelope.

Strengthening the Outline

Now you are ready to examine the contents of each chapter envelope, ordering your ideas to produce a well-organized chapter. Develop an outline for each chapter, using the same procedures. Examine these outlines: Do they create interest? Do they withhold information long enough to create tension? Do they plant the germs for later conflict? Do they foreshadow what might be ahead? Do your characters show us who they are by what they say, think, or do? Are your antagonists identifiable people? Do they want something just as badly as your protagonists? Are both formidable enough to sustain credibility in their accomplishments? And, most important of all, do your chapters have a beginning, a middle and an ending that makes us want to turn the pages and continue reading?

Planning Your Episodes

Examine the beginning of the first and subsequent episodes. Are the episodes fully developed, each containing a crisis that carries us into the next episode and the next? The first chapter must grab the reader. It must also lead into the first episode, which must then join with the other episodes at key points, heightening or expanding the story's frame, explaining what has come before or foreshadowing more excitement ahead.

Perhaps you have noticed critical gaps that must be closed with essential plot information. You may need a flashback or an obligatory incident to give credibility to an action. In some cases, you will need to split the contents of an envelope, making two chapters. Make notes in pencil on the envelope covers about the changes occuring as the plot thickens. When all chapters have been examined and outlines are complete, put the book aside and give it time to ripen further in your mind. No matter how tightly you weave your episodes, new ideas will present themselves, and you will want to go back to your outlines.

At this point you should be able to tell who will be the best viewpoint character for telling the story—a single, first-person viewpoint or multiple viewpoints as the plot materializes. Experience will also show that, when you begin the actual writing of the book, you will stray from the outline, creating more exciting situations with greater story impact. At the same time, your characters and events will become real-to-life.

Building Unified Patterns

Before you begin pulling your story together, examine the following three methods writers have used to ensure unity from beginning to final resolution. Decide which method you feel most comfortable with when plotting and writing your novel.

1. Build unity by plotting episodes that are dependent upon each other. Here we are speaking of unity of action. Events in one episode depend upon the action that has preceded it, and they are directly related to the actions that

follow in the next episode. If a single episode is cut from your novel, the chain of events will be broken, and the breach must be mended. You will find an example of this unifying technique in Jane Austin's *Pride and Prejudice.* Get a copy of this novel and examine it carefully.[1]

2. Build a chain of life episodes to allow us to follow your principal character as he/she sets out to accomplish something spectacular. We follow his/her escapades with close attention and much delight.[2] Examine the plots of Charles Dickens—more specifically, *David Copperfield.* The title names the character whose life leads us into a number of humorous and tragic situations involving a variety of interesting people.

3. Build a unity in related episodes that, though not dependent upon the action in previous episodes, begin and end on the right track.[3] An example of unity in related episodes is found in Mark Twain's *Adventures of Huckleberry Finn.* Huck's adventures take him among some interesting characters in episodes with various settings along the Mississippi. Of course Huck is primarily concerned about the runaway slave, Jim, and he earnestly tries to help Jim reach the free port of Cairo in a free state. This thread never leaves us and is the central point where most episodes begin and end. The principal difference between this method and the dependent episode method is in the body of the episodes. Mark Twain uses the events taking place in the middle of these episodes to characterize Huck, Jim, and the best and worst of a medley of characters who represent life on the Mississippi. Examine this novel, and compare the episodic linkage with those found in *Pride and Prejudice.*

More About Plotting

Novels don't come to you full-bloom, as sometimes happens in a short story. Novelists watch their work grow painstakingly, as they paint the magic that comes from the first idea and build upon it until completion of the manuscript. Often, the journey is punctuated by moments of despair.[4]

Phyllis Whitney used new setting as her springboard to get her into writing a book. She had experienced China, Japan, and the Philippines early in life, but she began by writing about New York, Hollywood, and other places that sounded glamorous to her. Eventually, she stumbled on some advice most professionals offer the novice: Write about what you know.[5]

She began a story set at a pineapple plantation she had known about in the Philippines. The story sold, but she learned in the process that her setting had been seen through the eyes of a child. She began traveling and researching backgrounds for stories.[6] You only have to check the fiction stacks in your library to discover how successful she has become.

What Are the Financial Rewards?

Some writers earn enormous sums even before their books are written. Others write stories that bring little or no pay, but they have the satisfaction of having their work accepted and published. Most writers fall somewhere in between these groups, perhaps earning enough to support themselves comfortably or simply to supplement other income.[7]

A few writers have received stratospheric sums for their novels. Monies have poured in from best-seller earnings in the marketplace, from the tremendous sums paid for film and paperback rights, from book club selections, and from publishing and other rights in foreign markets. Only a few writers bring in blockbusters, which are promoted heavily by the conglomerates who often neglect the remainder of their lists to keep the bankroll swelling.[8] Still, writers continue to write the books they must write, driven along by a compelling desire to create exciting fiction and to see their work published.

Part Three
Analyses of Supportive Elements and Techniques

17

Plotting with Symbols

The American flag, raised on flag poles in front of government offices, post offices, schools, and other locations is displayed with pride. The stars, the blue field, and the thirteen red and white stripes are symbols representing the birth of our nation, its growth, and the character of its people. The symbols help bond our people together with a strong national pride.

Writers use *familiar symbols* to serve several useful purposes: (1) to accent the theme; (2) to parallel a key event in the story; (3) to create a special mood; (4) to serve as a resolving device—an event that is linked directly with the resolution made at the conclusion; or (5) to foreshadow a plot event.

Some familiar symbols are:

flags	barber poles
tides	black cats
birds	skulls & crossbones
ships	Thanksgiving turkey
rings	snakes
bridges	a rose
a heart	fire
crosses	the moor
the Star	the moon

Guidelines for Selecting Symbols

The number and choices of symbols an author may use are almost unlimited, but there are certain guidelines you will want to consider when using them.[1]

1. Symbols must serve a purpose.

2. They must be familiar to everyone.

3. They must fit easily and naturally into the action or forward movement of the story.

Five Purposes for Using Symbols

There are five purposes for using symbols.[2]

1. A symbol might be used throughout the length of a story to accent the theme. For example, "The Fall of the House of Usher," by Edgar Allen Poe, uses the house and the crack in the walls of the house as symbols for the deterioration of the souls who dwell in the house. As the plot deepens, evil destruction is repeatedly foreshadowed; the crack widens and lengthens until the house and the souls within are

destroyed. Symbols thus accent the theme: Evil passions destroy men's souls.

2. The symbol can parallel key events in the story. In "Dr. Heidegger's Experiment," by Nathaniel Hawthorne, the rose is used as a symbol. Dr. Heidegger invites four of his friends, three men and a woman, to his home for an experiment. The four aged souls are curious about their invitations, and as the story unfolds they become exuberant. The strange doctor has in his possession a vase of water taken from the Fountain of Youth in Florida. He takes a pressed, withered rose (symbolic of their aging) and places it in the vase of water. The rose is quickly restored to its former beauty. They give little attention to the doctor's suggestion about rules to guide and protect them through the perils of youth. They drink the water and become young again, but they then repeat the foolish, sinful ways of their youths. A fight breaks out over the Widow Wycherly. The vase tips, and the remaining water is lost. The rose slowly fades again and withers, and the four return to their old, wrinkled former selves. The symbol has followed the key events, providing a visual parallel to changes in the characters.

3. The symbol might be used to create a special mood. Gothic novels use a number of symbols, each adding to the mood. The moor is a symbol of dreariness, loneliness, and mysteriousness. Storms foreshadow evil lurking about. Wolves, dogs, or other animals howl, bark, hoot, wail, adding to the sense of mystery, loneliness, suspense, and fear.

4. The symbol might be used in two symbolic incidents; the first incident parallels the problem or conflict, and the second includes a significant revelation that foreshadows how the problem is resolved at the end. Like a seed, the first symbolic incident is planted close to the beginning of the

story, and the second symbolic incident, with a significant new development or change, is planted just before the climax. Let us say a child is watching "Animal Kingdom" on television. Her mother, aware of her daughter's interest, stops her work to see what is happening on the screen. A lioness is nursing her newborn cubs, occasionally taking her paw and pulling one closer so she can clean its body with her tongue (the first incident). The mother goes back to her work feeling pleased about her daughter's interest. Twelve years later, the mother is faced with an important decision. Her daughter has finished high school and wants to enroll in a college far from home. The woman is reminded of the terrible things that might happen to the girl when she is no longer under the immediate protection of her home and parents. She suggests they take some time to think about the decision. Ironically, a week later, the mother finds the daughter watching a special program sponsored by National Geographic. On the screen, a lioness turns on her overgrown cubs, swatting them with her paw when they try to nurse (the second incident). Shortly afterwards, the daughter is told she can go to the college of her choice. She must be given a chance to make decisions for herself to learn to make it on her own.[3] The symbolic incidents here, of course, include the mother-cub relationships at birth and at weaning time.

5. A symbol might be used to foreshadow a crucial moment, perhaps the climax of the story. For example, "The Scarlet Ibis," by James Hurst, uses a storm and a scarlet ibis to such good effects. The setting is a Kansas farm. The story is told in first person, major character's point-of-view. The narrator is looking back upon his childhood with deep regrets. When a second child, the narrator's brother, was born, the narrator knew he had a big problem. The doctor said the child

might not live. But he did. The older brother gave the child a name that stuck—Doodles—for, before the child could walk, he moved backwards on his hands and knees like a doodlebug. When it was apparent that the older boy would have to go to school with a brother who could not walk or run like other children, he grew ashamed and reveled in false pride. The false pride paved a rough road of heartrending conflict, driving the narrator to commit a number of cruel deeds that frightened the brother. In the course of these stressful efforts to make Doodles walk, run, and row a boat, the child learned to stand and eventually to walk. Through it all, Doodles never protested much more than, "Please don't hurt me, brother." He loved his older brother deeply.

One day a storm approached. Doodles was in the yard and saw the great scarlet ibis settle into the treetop. The family, sensing the excitement, came outside to investigate. The father explained that the bird was blown off course by the great storm. (Here is the planting of the symbol that will parallel the final event.) The scarlet ibis plunges to the earth and lies there, its neck broken, and its tiny, fragile legs crossed in death.

The final scene finds the two boys racing for the house as a storm catches them at play, the rain coming down in torrents. They have spent the morning in Old Woman Swamp, definitely off course for the weaker Doodles who is unable to keep up with his brother. The narrator suddenly realizes that the boy is not behind him. He calls. No answer. Later, he discovers Doodles lying in a clump of grass, driven beyond his endurance. His neck has been broken. The brother sees his fallen ibis and realizes how much he loves him—too late. False pride had blinded him to what was real and important.

Recognizing Symbols

Any serious writer knows the importance of recognizable symbols whose meanings can be readily interpreted. Without a clear meaning, the symbol becomes confusing or, at best, nothing more than an image with its own, momentary significance, which then is gone. Symbols must have a distinct, clear purpose and must be easily recognizable by the readers. Remember, the first responsibility of a writer is to write for your readers; keep them in mind always.

Studying symbols must be done with a reasonable amount of caution. Critics have sometimes carried their analyses too far and have found symbols where authors insist none were intended. Their search for the hidden meanings of certain objects or in natural occurrences may lead us far from an author's intent and into a fabrication of meanings born in fertile, imaginative minds. Such can happen to anyone who begins to see symbols in everything that is written.[4]

Symbols can be in any fictional genre. Writers and students of literature quickly sense them when they are used with genuine, underlying purposes; they seldom fail to accomplish for the author an indelible imprint of sharply focused images and themes that live indefinitely in the minds of their readers.

The moor in *Jane Eyre,* with its stark, mysterious atmosphere, is unforgettable. Still, it is not the moor, nor the storms, nor the wolves howling in the darkness that make these things symbols; it is the quality of life and events, that parallel or follow these descriptions that give them their identity and reference as symbols.[5]

For example, a setting enriched with the introduction of a storm, a witch's moon, or any other distinct mood-setting image, paves the way for a frightening event or the reappearance of an old threat. Such symbolic descriptions in *Wuthering Heights* prepare us for the appearance of that stormy character, Heathcliff, and for the mysterious circumstances surrounding his sudden departure and reappearance.

Developing Your Own Symbols

Before selecting any symbols you might want to use, you will already need to have decided:

1. What is going to happen in the story, and to whom;

2. Who will tell your story;

3. What strengths your protagonist has;

4. What weaknesses in your protagonist make us fear that he/she will fail.

5. What strengths your antagonist has that contrasts with the protagonist and that allows for a formidable opposition;

6. Whether the conflict is a life-and-death struggle or about a character's transformation in outlook and character;

7. What setting will fit the action in each incident, allowing your readers to feel that they are there watching every move;

8. How the weaknesses of your protagonist will spur a predictable surge of ability, talent, or knowledge hinted upon earlier; and

9. What message or underlying idea readers will get from your story (theme).

At this point, write a synopsis of your story. If you're planning a novel, list major incidents under each chapter heading. The headings, even if discarded later will lend direction to your novel, taking it from the beginning and leading logically to the end. Now you are ready to investigate what symbols will serve one or more of the five purposes explained earlier in this chapter. If you do find appropriate symbols, make notes in the margins of your synopsis, designating the first and subsequent placements of the symbols and their references.

Your symbol can be included in the title, as in "The Scarlet Ibis"; however, you must also plant it in the story proper, perhaps among the descriptive passages on setting or in a special symbolic situation written specifically to foreshadow or parallel some other key part of the story. In each instance, the symbol should be easy for the reader to spot, once the formative reference has been made, and it should be something familiar to him.

Symbol: The Planting and the Reference

The bird, which had been blown off course by a storm, later plummeted from the top of the tree to the earth below. This incident is merely a tragic descriptive event until the final scene where Doodles lies in a clump of weeds in the midst of a storm. The symbol is planted, then, when the ibis plummets to earth, and we are told that the storm has blown it out of the regions it normally inhabits. The beautiful bird with the delicate neck and limbs becomes a tragic symbol, a parallel to the story's climax. The symbol's purpose, however, is uncovered in the stormy scene where Doodles is found dead in a clump of grass, his neck broken.

Symbolic Plants

The prologue from a partially plotted novel, *Summer of the Owl* (specifically developed for this text), is used here to show how symbolic plants can arouse reader interest by foreshadowing conflict, even before the story begins. Later, you will see how follow-up references to these plants will give these symbols legitimate purposes. This prologue includes a number of symbolic plants: the chains binding Serena; Charlie, the owl; the hawk; and the rattlesnake. Perhaps you noted that one symbol, the owl, appears in the title. As you read the prologue, try to determine who or what these symbols might represent.

SUMMER OF THE OWL

Prologue:

A small clearing appeared in front of Josh. In its center, the firetower stood tall above young pine saplings forming the perimeter of its sandy base. He grew uneasy. Somebody was up there in the dark cabin watching every move he made. He just had that queer feeling, and, before he could decide what made him feel the way he did, a light above the cabin began flashing and rotating like the bright red light of a fire truck.

A light shone faintly inside the cabin, barely illuminating the windows. The face and hands now pressing against the dirty pane were shadowy, vague impressions.

An ominous sound came from inside the cabin.

"Go back, Josh! Go back . . . !

A dark cloud mushroomed and consumed everything before him but the tower. He found himself standing at the base of its steel supports. He looked up, grabbed the steel hand rails, and took the first step; felt the steps move under him. He steadied himself. The steps had become an escalator!

The entrance in the cabin floor above him opened at the center and swung back on its hinges, silent, as though what he saw was a film set in slow motion. A dizziness threatened to overcome him. He grabbed the steel hand rails with a firm grip to steady himself. He did not look down.

Serena looked down at him through the poorly lighted opening, her head slumped forward, with her long black hair falling tragically forward. "Go back, Josh!" Her voice was sterner this time.

He saw the heavy iron chains that bound her. An oversized lock suspended from the chain pulled at her waist. She, in turn, pulled and shook both lock and chain in fits of obvious distress.

Her forlorn figure began to fade.

"Don't go!" he cried. But no sound left his lips. A strange power had made him mute.

In a fragment of a second, he was standing beside her in the small cabin. She flashed a grin, and he read the cruelty in it.

"There!" she shrieked triumphantly. She extended a slender arm, pointed a finger downward toward the small clearing.

He felt the dizziness return. He shook his head to clear it, then he reached for the lock.

She pushed him back toward the dirty glass pane. "You can't help me, Josh. Nobody can help me now. I've lost the key. I had it once . . . and now it's gone." She drew back and wept.

Josh felt the knot tying up his stomach. He glanced downward, felt the rising acrophobia and steadied himself again. . . .

The scene changed. He stood beside a dark, open grave. He heard the sound a shovel makes when it's driven into a soft mound of freshly dug earth. Brick Gardener was beside him, standing at the head of the grave. His friend gazed solemnly into its darkness. "Did you see the hawk?"

"No." Josh felt a foreboding spirit surrounding him.

"Just flew right over," Brick said. "Saw what was happenin'

down here and didn't do nothing about it. Look down there. See for yourself. It's too late to help that dummy."

A wavering light shone from behind Josh.

"Carmella? What's wrong?"

She was dressed in black. Her heavy, round figure drew in closer to the grave, holding a flickering flambeau above their heads. "The hawk got too much on his mind, Brick. Everybody wanta tell the hawk what he got to do. You can't tell a hawk what to do. He got to know how to survive, too."

"What bird?" Josh asked.

"He's gone now. Never gonna see 'im around when you you need 'im. Go on, Josh. Bury the dummy." Brick offered him the shovel. "Go ahead. He dug the hole hisself, Josh. He's crazy! Stickin' his nose into territory don't belong to 'im. Bury 'im!"

"Bury him, Josh!" Serena's voice shrieked from the tower.

"No," Josh said. "Put some light here, Carmella."

"I'm sorry, Josh. I know how much you loved your friend." She moved in with the light. "There," she whispered. "Can you see him?"

It was dark inside the grave, even with Carmella's light. Josh went down on his hands and knees. . . . "It's Charlie!" He looked up at Brick, and then at Carmella. "What's he doing here?"

"He just another stupid owl who ain't so smart," Brick answered. "You saw what was happenin' all along. You . . . you coulda stopped 'im."

"He was hungry, Brick."

"Greedy," Brick said. The light from the flambeau lent a bronze tint to the youth's cinnamon-colored skin.

"You never liked the owl," Josh said. "You've never tried to understand him." He lay flat on his stomach so that he could reach the owl and snatch him from the grave.

But Charlie was in trouble! A large, slick-skinned rattlesnake was in a corner of the depths, coiled and ready to strike. His jaws stood agape, exposing his deadly fangs.

Josh cried out and jerked back from the hole. He straightened up, grabbed Brick's shovel.

Serena's laughter pierced the darkness.

Josh stopped, threw the shovel aside. Where was Charlie? The rattlesnake lay dead at the foot of a shadowy image. Someone was lying there where the owl had been, his shirt sleeve torn and bloodied.

Josh's face turned grim. He looked down into the face of Jen Roman!

"It's Jen!" he cried. And again he was mute.

He searched the space around him. Everyone and everything had been consumed by the blackness. All that remained was a clammy cold and an emptiness that clung to him and left him feeling helpless. . . .

Within the prologue, five significant symbols have been planted:

1. The chains that hold Serena in bondage
2. Charlie, the owl
3. The hawk
4. The rattlesnake
5. The firetower

Each of these must refer to specific events that will take place as the story progresses. These later incidents will become symbolic references, which clarify the meanings and purposes for the symbols.

Psychologists tell us that dreams about someone we know in bondage might actually signify the reverse scenario: Actually, we are the ones bound or limited by that person. Here is one of Josh's problems. His aunt has returned to live with him and his father, the school principal, after having been away for four years. She left when Josh was twelve. Now he is sixteen and was about to become a junior at Metcalfe High. He isn't a kid any longer.

The owl represents his friend, Jen Roman. Jen is an aggressive senior ready to make his mark in the world. In the course of the story, he disappears. The hawk represents an evasive and cautious Chief Meadows, Lake Warren's new chief of police. The rattlesnake represents an evil, destructive plot being woven by two sinister collaborators in Gaston City, the county seat.

Josh has acrophobia, an abnormal dread of heights. The firetower symbol accents a weakness of our protagonist, who must eventually overcome his phobia to save Jen's life.

The Plot

This is planned as a young adult mystery novel of forty to fifty thousand words, or 180-200 typewritten pages. It is to be divided into twenty chapters, nine to ten pages each.

Let's plot some additional possibilities for this novel. Let's say, that although Serena's departure had confused and hurt Josh, it was the change he noticed in her when she came back to Lake Warren that confused and hurt him most of all. She had been a warm, supportive woman of simple dress and manner. Now she wore expensive clothes and spent the better part of her time with the wealthier families in this small textile village.

She had also become a shrew, attacking his choice of friends, even those she had never met. She makes his efforts to find Jen very difficult. His love for the woman who had been a mother to him for twelve years, versus his concern for Jen Roman's safety makes up the major conflicts Josh faces.

Now let's turn to Brick. Brick, his neighbor and trusted friend, is also Jen's competition for the honors to be had with the Metcalfe Lions' football team. Brick never becomes as close to Jen, as Josh does, until the climax of the novel. Brick brings out the worst and best in Josh, allowing us to identify closely with the protagonist; he provides a contrasting opinion of Jen Roman, supported by the Aunt, and becomes an antagonist until the conclusion when Jen saves his life at the near-expense of losing his own.

Josh is incensed when the chief of police (the hawk) orders him away from Bird Island. When Josh offers clues linking certain important figures with criminal activities in and around Lake Warren, the chief appears to ignore him.

One after another, events occur in or around the mill village that confound Josh and his friends. Later, Jen's adventurous spirit takes him beyond the everyday life of a graduating senior, into the territory of criminals who have different plans for the textile village. Then he disappears.

The dialogue presented in Chapter 10 to illustrate a variety of fiction elements also contained symbolic references to several of the symbols introduced in the prologue. Reread the prologue and follow with the incident in Chapter 10. Where would be the correct placement of this reference incident in the hypothetical novel we are studying? Since tensions are evident in Josh's behavior in the field, the incident will probably fit well in Chapter 3 of the novel, where we will want to jolt reader interest.

That chapter might also be an appropriate time for Jen to disappear, Josh already having become suspicious of the black limousine he saw following Jen when his friend returned his van. Josh had then recognized Chief Meadow's police car in front of the high school, and his plans for an exciting weekend going fishing on Lake Warren are threatened by the chief's interrogation in his father's office. Jen disappears and Josh recalls the bloodied arm in the dream. A strong emotional crisis develops from this point.

Adding Other Plot Elements

The novel will develop in carefully selected incidents chosen to fill in the gaps, to strengthen characterizations, and to advance the plot in an exciting pace. We might first summarize ideas for the plot, then, we can produce an orderly sequence of these by making notes on the fronts and backs of the appropriate chapter envelopes. For example, the following ideas might be summarized, then, noted:

1. Josh is regularly disappointed in Brick who takes a negative view of Josh's friendship and support for Jen; however, an incident at the lake leaves Brick confused, for clues uncovered at the boathouse leave strong evidence that Jen might be working with the police. Still, Brick refuses to change his attitude about Brick's criminal connections until the climax when Jen appears and saves his life. But Jen is captured and taken away. Brick joins forces with Josh to find Jen and set him free.

2. In the final chapter, Josh will overcome his "height sickness" to get to the senior before he dies from his injuries.

3. The problem with his aunt will become reconciled when Josh discovers the exciting clue, wedged in a crack on the stair lift in his home. He finds a photo of his aunt with a

small child, a girl about three years old, seated on the front steps of his grandparents' home in Savannah. The significance of this photo does not come to light until after Brick's life is saved. Josh senses the truth. His aunt left because she was carrying the child. Her brother (Josh's father) is the principal at Metcalfe High. Serena didn't want to hurt or embarrass Josh or his father.

4. Josh is able to put several plans into operation, with the help of Carmella—plans that do not appear to work until the very end. He comes face-to-face with the man that he believes is the girl's father. The man is a television repairman who has repaired their sets on at least two occasions. Josh mentions his aunt having returned to Lake Warren. He shows the man the girl's picture.

5. Serena's romance with Mr. Big turns sour. Josh has raised doubts in her mind about him. An investigation of her own leads her to an important discovery: Her boyfriend is building a drug base on Bird Island, and she has been wrong about his interest in her. But all ends well for her and her daughter when the child's father acts to claim her and the child for his own.

Other exciting events concerning Jen's girlfriend, a missing van, an unconscious man found in the woods near the falls, an attempt on Josh's life at the fishing camp, a secret landing, and a dozen other suspenseful situations, can be made more meaningful and memorable through symbols and continued references to them throughout the plot.

Unfortunately, ideas do not come to us in ready-made order; therefore, the next big step is to include brief notations of these incidents in their appropriate chapter outlines. When all loose ends are filled and you are satisfied that you have a workable plot, start writing.

Plotting is fun. Too often, students do not spend time on this important pre-writing stage. Knowing where you are going, having several ideas sketched out for key incidents, having your principal characters firmly set in your head, and developing a willingness to write and rewrite are minimal requirements in the early stages of writing creatively.

All stories do not have symbols, but those that do will include some of the most memorable stories you and I will ever read.

18

Developing Effective Dialogues

Dialogue is the most effective support element a writer of fiction or nonfiction has available. Readers are quick to note the amount of dialogue in the pages of a novel or in the length of a short story or a magazine article before they decide to read it.

Dialogue can include every key element one needs for telling a story, and it provides these essentials in palatable dosages. The reader delights in characters who come alive in conversations that reveal who and what they are, as well as what they are up to and why.

Dialogue becomes the novelist's best friend when he is faced with completing a book of two hundred or so pages. Obviously, conversations use up more space and take far less writing than do paragraphs of exposition. You are consequently encouraged to master the development of effective dialogues and to use them as often as you can.[1]

One important point must be made here, however: Dialogue must have purposes, and its development must be managed with knowledge and skill. One value of dialogue is a visual contrast to solid blocks of expository writing, but it must be written clearly and informatively, imparting essential information. Frequently, beginners stop the action of their story and let their characters chat for a time about nonessentials. Professional writers learn to make each line of dialogue achieve a specific effect: characterization, mood, conflict, and other elements are woven into the spoken words.[2]

What Dialogues Can Tell

When story people are involved in conversation, several good things can happen for your story:

1. We enjoy hearing the characters talk. We enjoy the faster pace of conversation.

2. We can sense anger, happiness, regrets, frustration, and descriptive details that draw our attention to what has happened, what is going to happen, or what is happening now.

3. Characters become full-fledged, real-life people, like those we know and those we've learned to dislike.

4. We might get a glimpse of the setting and sense the mood of the people.

5. We might get a "thematic" reference. Remember the words of the lawyer in "Bartleby" (Chapter 12)? The biblical reference to the Old Testament casts a revealing light upon the theme.

6. We might get a "symbolic" reference. In "The Scarlet Ibis" (Chapter 17), by James Hurst, the presence of the scarlet ibis is explained by Doodles' father. This symbolic plant foreshadows and parallels the closing incident. When the older brother turns back to find Doodles, the reader senses the foreboding signals of the final, dramatic scene:

> I began to weep, and the tear-blurred vision in red before me looked very familiar. "Doodles!" I screamed above the pounding storm and threw my body to the earth above him. For a long time, it seemed forever, I lay there crying, sheltering my fallen ibis from the heresy of rain.

Action and Mood

When dialogues contain descriptive references to what characters do (action) and in what manner it is done (mood), the writer has included classic bits of "business." According to D. C. Fontana, former editor of "Star Trek," these bits of business can include "a look, a move, a facial expression, a tone of voice, a mood, a pause in speech. As such, then, it differs from long action sequences like car chases and fights in which dialogue is minimal or nonexistent."[3]

To give you a clear picture of what "business" does for your dialogue, here are two illustrations:

(Without business)

> "Mama?"
> "What do you want, Charles?"
> "It's going to rain."
> "You're certain?"
> "I'm certain."
> "Charles? Charles? Charles!"

Here the characters are indentified through the use of nouns in direct address. What does either character feel about the other? about the possibilities of rain? The dialogue doesn't tell us.

(With business)

> "Mama?" Both hands pressed deeply into his coat pocket, he stared at the floor.
>
> "What do you want, Charles?" She didn't look up from her crocheting.
>
> "It's going to rain." He shifted his weight from one sneaker to the other, glanced at his watch, and then at her. His shoulders slumped. Why didn't she say something? She knew how important the jam session was for him. At breakfast, he had told her he might even get to sit in with the band, show them what a great sax man he was.
>
> "You're certain?" She reached up and turned the lampshade to get more light on her work, fingered the pattern with apparent satisfaction.
>
> "I'm certain."
>
> She knew, but did not offer to take him there. Without another word, without looking at her, he stormed to his room and slammed the door shut.
>
> The woman looked up. "Charles? Charles? Charles!"

From this exchange, we can see that, at first, the mother appears indifferent about the rain and the jam session. Obviously, Charles sees this as a lack of caring for him. He is frustrated when she does not offer to take him to the session. Of course, he has failed to recognize her deep concentration in the crocheting pattern, one that requires counting each movement of the needle. The goal of the moment for each is in conflict. Yet, when she becomes aware of the situation, she is concerned.

The business of action and mood presents the atmosphere within a frame of dialogue. (Earlier, you learned how atmosphere includes the action, the mood, and the setting.) You also receive necessary information for identifying with one or both of these characters. From such tags of business and dialogue, emotions surface, and conflict is quickly felt. From this short dialogue, you have learned that the setting is inside the home in a den or living room. Other information could be added if the setting or its characters have not been sufficiently described previously. Note also that the conversation does not include "he/she said." They were not essential. The paragraphing and nouns in direct address help us keep tabs on who is talking, acting and feeling.

What Thoughts Can Tell Us

The thoughts of characters and their spoken words, supplied by first person accounts or by third person, omniscient storytellers, provide readers with the pertinent details they will need for story analysis and for personal enjoyment. But when you include the thoughts of your viewpoint characters, keep in mind that the readers prefer that the writer remains outside the story.

Writer intrusion:

> Richard's friends have turned against him. What can he do to regain their support?

Improved:

> My friends have turned against me, Richard thought. I must do something to regain their support.

The more dialogue and thoughts a writer uses, the better able we are to identify with the story people; however, there are governing rules one should follow. To make the dialogue sound right, the words must fit the characters who speak them. The queen of England would appear ridiculous saying, "If we're goin' to whup the daylight outa Phillip, we orta git Drake over here and go over our plans."

Character, Atmosphere, Conflict, and Plot

Again, dialogue must have purpose. The plot must move forward; we must be able to identify with the characters and the problems they face. In addition, we want to know where everything is taking place. In the extended dialogue, the writer is able to show and tell, giving major characters an opportunity to show themselves and allowing the storyteller an opportunity to narrate or tell some things.

> Change of Heart
>
> Princess Elena strolled in the garden among rhododendrons, lilacs, and varicolored patches of verbena edging the narrow walk. On her left, where the lawn sloped gently toward the Thames, a bronze statue of Henry VIII, greening with age, stood stout and pompous on its marble pedestal.
>
> "Pss-sst!"
>
> "Albert?" The young Prince Albert's study was to her right. She paused. The draperies were drawn. Twenty, and he was still such a child, she thought. When would he grow up?

"Elena . . ."

She shifted her attention to the thick growth of evergreen shrubs below the window.

"Albert?" Her brother had not joined the king and queen at breakfast. He had not heard the latest reports from the continent.

"Don't look back, Elena . . . please. Father may be watching."

"Ridiculous!" she said. "What are you up to? Father's furious about your behavior!"

"He promised!"

"Promised? Promised what? Promises can't always be kept." She began moving away from his voice, pretending to be interested in the chimney swifts flying in fast-changing directions across the cool September sky.

"Wait!" he said. "He . . . Father's out of his mind." He stepped from behind the evergreens, a blond youth with a slim, straight frame. "He insisted . . . well, you've heard him Elena. He talks of nothing but that fat Austrian baggage. Insists I marry Princess Sophia. Elena . . . I . . . I won't do it!"

She slipped an arm under his and led him across the green lawn toward the queen's rose garden. There were a few late blooms. "There may be a war," she said. "Austrian brigades are holding skirmishes near their borders with our allies."

"I never meddle with politics," he said. "You should have been a prince, Elena. You know so much about those things."

Elena withdrew her arm and wheeled to face him. His brows were drawn with discontent. Such a hopeless adventurer, she thought. "Albert, we must talk about it."

"Father could stop it," he said. He took one quick look backward toward the king's chamber window. "England is strong, Elena."

"A marriage would bring the proud old Austrian to his senses."

"I won't do it!"

"You will," she said, turning out of the garden and down the sloping green toward the Thames. A late morning fog hung over the water, and the autumn air was cooler than she had anticipated. "You should have joined us for breakfast. Father explained what was happening in Central Europe."

"I need money, Elena. I could go to Paris. I have friends in Paris. Help me, Elena . . . help me get away."

"You haven't heard, Albert?" She turned to meet the forlorn look upon his face. The sight saddened her. He must have gone without sleep for some time.

"I'm not ready for marriage, Elena. Besides, I've heard it from reliable sources that the woman is every bit of thirty!"

"Twenty-four!"

"But I'm eighteen!"

"Your fat little Austrian baggage is about to become Queen Sophia of Venubia."

His face brightened. "Oh? How did she manage that?"

"Her dear uncle Joseph choked on a T-bone. No heirs. The throne goes to his brother's only child, a daughter."

"The king of Austria?"

"His daughter . . . Princess Sophia."

"Would the king invade her country?"

"No. Others have their eyes on Venubia. Sophia favors annexation with her father. Unmarried. Too close to her father."

"Then why have a war?"

"The Magyars would protest annexation . . . would rather fight."

"Did Father know this last evening?" He brushed a blond lock from his troubled face.

He hasn't shaved, Elena noticed. "No, the courier arrived just this morning."

"Venubia must have a handsome treasury."

"The king was thrifty."

"Stingy," Albert said. And after a pause, "I'd have to give up a lot. I couldn't travel the way I like."

He's coming around, she decided. "You would have a great responsibility to your new country. The prince consort would have important duties to perform. You would certainly become a key minister . . . perhaps minister of the navy. Your duties would require more travel than you have ever experienced."

"Sophia really has rich possibilities, don't you agree?"

"Oh, yes. Very."

"Maybe Father isn't as crazy as I thought," Albert said. "Sophia's attractive in some ways."

"A simple beauty," she said. It was not easy to maintain her serious composure.

"Beauty isn't everything," he said.

"A prince has responsibilities."

"I should pay my respects . . . to the queen."

"Absolutely . . . and to Sophia. By the way, Father has made the arrangements. We'll accompany him and Mother on the trip to Venubia City. Father says we must attend the state funeral services for the unfortunate king."

"Unfortunate . . . yes. When?"

"Four days. You have four days to decide what you must."

"Father thinks of everything!"

"You should try to eat," Elena said.

"I'm starved!"

Elena beamed with victory.

When conflict develops your characters begin to breathe on their own; they begin to act out the roles you have given them; you may feel them pulling on the reins and moving away on their own. If you do, hold tight, stopping to reread the words they have spoken, tempering or cutting words that slow the pace or lead in other directions.

Though the previous excerpt—drawn to illustrate dialogue with essential story elements—does not have much of a plot, the dialogue reveals a gay, childlike quality and certain naiveté in Albert, while his sister, Princess Elena, is patronizing, knowledgeable, and understanding. Most of the conversation produces a humorous note, but Elena's thoughts could be applied at the end of this fragment to take us further, foreshadowing trouble ahead not only for England but also for her brother and for Venubia. Perhaps an ambitious Austrian prince will set in motion an intriguing web of conflict, challenging the weak prince consort. If this is to be the case, a seed for that intrigue will have to be planted earlier in the plot.

Objective Viewpoint

Hemingway's story, "Hills Like White Elephants," uses dialogue in an objective, third person point-of-view, leaving the reader to interpret what the problems and details are. He does not interlace a great deal of descriptive narrative with the spoken words.

> "You've got to realize," he said, "that I don't want you to do it if you don't want to. I'm perfectly willing to go through with it if it means anything to you."

Of course, the man is speaking with a forked tongue. He becomes the antagonist, a heel with no evidence of humanity. He wants her to have an abortion. The author does not bother to tell us this; he doesn't have to. Every word that spills forth from the man's mouth reinforces the reader's perceptions of a selfish, unfeeling character. The effect is powerful.

And what does the woman's response tell us?

> "Doesn't it mean anything to you? We could get along."

Again, character comes to the surface without a third person narration of it. Dialogue does it better. The woman is holding on to a grain of hope that she will be allowed to keep the child, and she wants the man who fathered it. But her hope fades with the reality borne upon the man's crushing response: "I don't want anyone else."

The cards are now on the table. What the antagonist wants and what he often implies about her having an abortion are tempered with cruel irony; the woman is faced with an agonizing choice, her own words laced with irony; the symbolic barren land on both sides of the station is used to press home a stirring, controversial theme.

Identifying the Speakers

Dialogues that fail to identify the speakers are rare; what beginners more often overlook are the possibilities for adding a variety of approaches to their character identifications. Anything repeated excessively becomes tiresome in fiction. We therefore ought to examine how we can vary this task.

> John studied Ella's responses to the radio report and grew suspicious. "You knew Victor Wayne?"
>
> "I knew him. Everybody knew Victor Wayne," she said.
>
> "I didn't . . . until now."
>
> "Most people then . . . not people like you. People who become workaholics."
>
> "What's that supposed to mean?"
>
> "John!"

Approach: Two characters, John and Ella are identified in the beginning of this third person, limited omniscient point-of-view. An additional reference, "she," has been used to help readers keep up with the changes in speakers.

Purposes for the dialogue: This one uncovers John's jealousy and suspicion about Ella and another man. We learn he is a workaholic, which may explain the causes for any tensions developing between them. It also shows us that Ella is alerted to his suspicions and is quick to respond.

The Verb "Said"

"Said" is a popular, effective action verb used with identifying nouns and pronouns. As mentioned earlier, some dialogues rely upon nouns in direct address or upon descriptive tags that identify the speakers following or preceding their words. Let's examine a brief dialogue that relies upon a balance of these identifiers and the use of "said":

> "It was a foolish thing for Tom to do," Tammy said. "What will happen to him, George?"
>
> "They arrested Tom this morning. Banged on the door at three in the morning. . . . He told me they crashed in like storm troopers, went over his belongings in a wild search for evidence."
>
> Tammy sat up in bed. "They found nothing?"
>
> "Just the diary." George shook his slippers from his feet.
>
> "Diary? Tom kept a diary?" she asked.
>
> "Kept a record of all transactions," he said. "I thought you knew that."
>
> "I didn't! Up! Get up, George! We've got to get hold of that diary!"

Again, the verb "said," when not used in the extreme, is an excellent companion for your identifying noun or pronoun. Sometimes, though, you will want to supply a substitute—when questions are asked, or when a substitute will give us an exact feel for the dialogue.

Here are some good substitutes you might want to consider:

reported	exclaimed
yelled	answered
declared	cried
squealed	shrieked
announced	retorted
observed	recalled
repeated	prattled
stuttered	argued

Check the dialogues of professional writers. For brief, tightly drawn imagery and plot details, examine several short stories. In the novel, although the dialogues concisely reflect the writer's purposes for them, you may find more fully developed story elements and techniques within a dialogue because the novel is roomier. Study these and evaluate the effectiveness of the verbs. Does the author use "said" more than other verbs?

Finally, once you have become familiar with the choices available to you, practice writing dialogues using the methods of character identification introduced in this chapter. Discover for yourself the importance of having prior knowledge of plot before writing your practice dialogues. The plot gives you ideas for rich delineations of character, atmosphere, and conflict, or for foreshadowing future problems. Without these guiding influences, your characters easily slip into pointless chatter.

Counterpoint

Counterpoint is a terrific technique for adding body and excitement to your dialogues. This technique involves weaving several tracks of conversation into a single incident. Success with it requires study and practice to produce effectively. First, the plot must be absolutely clear to you. Divergent forces will be at work here, and confusion is almost certain to occur unless you know how these divergent forces will meet, what time is best for their juncture, and how each contrasting force will help us understand character, atmosphere, plot, and a medley of additional details.

Suppose our scene deals with two young people who are attending a New Year's Eve party. Sarah and Arnold are obviously uncomfortable, while around them, other young couples are dancing or chatting excitedly. Sarah is anxious and fidgety, unable to tell Arnold she wants to break off their engagement. We see her become angry with herself, causing her to display contempt for Arnold. Arnold feels the coolness, but maybe he attributes her behavior to something she ate. Besides, he's wrapped up with the spirit of the people and the music and the occasion.

Search for Sanity

"Let's dance, Sarah." Arnold let his hand rest on hers.

Sarah pulled her hand free. "Not now, Arnold." She wasn't looking at him. Her eyes were locked on the stage.

"Hey, Arnie!" Jim Penniweather yelled from across the ballroom. "Y'all havin' a wake?"

"Yes," Sarah said, barely moving her lips. No one heard her. Most of all, she wanted Arnold to know how she felt. But how could she tell him their romance was dead? Hadn't she always tried to laugh at his jokes and his silly pranks?

"Happy New Year!" Arnold yelled. He glanced across the table at Sarah, mimicked the singer, started beating out the rhythm on the table.

Sarah took a handkerchief from her purse and wiped her eyes. She felt she had to do something or else she would have to scream.

"You wanta dance?" asked Arnold. "The old year is about to die out. Gotta make way for the new."

How right you are, Sarah thought. But if she had tried to tell him that, he wouldn't have heard her. The floor vibrated with the loud music.

"You two come over and join us!" Sue Penniweather was standing beside their table, smiling, exposing her overbite of large, over-sized teeth. "Sarah?"

"We're having a wake," Sarah said.

"Wake?"

"The death of an affair."

"Come, Sarah," Arnold pleaded. "Let's get on the dance floor. Three minutes to midnight!"

"He's celebrating the old year," Sarah said.

"What about you?"

"I want to forget it."

"Hey, Arnie!" Jim Penniweather yelled. "Send my wife

back here and grab your woman . . ." The band struck up a new dance tune that drowned him out.

"Calling it quits?" Sue asked.

"Definitely. But look at him. I can't tell him that."

"I'll ask her." Arnold was standing beside the table now, slapping his palms to the rhythm of a new dance number. "Hi, Sue. What do you think? That skinny guy you came in with wants to dance."

"Jim's just like a kid." Sue grinned, waved to Jim, then turned back to Sarah. "Forever young, he says. I married him. . . . . thought I'd be able to change him." She pursed her lips. Smiled. Showed her overbite.

"A universal fault," Sarah said.

"It's that bad? Maybe you're coming down with something," Sue said. She shot a quick glance at Arnold. "Get Sarah and dance," she said, just moving her lips for him to read.

"Sue! Over here, Baby!" Jim motioned from the dance floor.

"It is that bad, Sue said. She shot another quick glance at Arnold, who now had his eyes on the cocktail waitress working her way to their table.

"Worse," Sarah said.

"Hey, sweetheart! Mama's here," the waitress said.

"Dance with Arnold, Sarah," Sue said. She looked at Arnold, "What do you say, Arnold?"

"He hasn't heard a word," Sarah said. Her full red lips pouted. "I could scream just knowing how close I came to getting hooked with that!"

"What's wrong?" Jim Penniweather had joined them. He looked at Arnold and then at Sarah, frowning.

The waitress removed the drinks from the tray and set them on the table. "Time to pay up, handsome."

Sarah grimaced.

"Hey, get with it, Sarah. A minute to go." Jim tried to smile, gave up, slipped a lean arm around Sue. "Anything holding you here?"

"Hey, handsome. Come off the cloud!" The waitress shouted above the music.

"What will you do?" Sue asked. They were reading lips now. The noises of voices and music reached a new high.

Arnold attempted a smile. He reached into his wallet and pulled out several bills, pressed them into the waitress's palm. "Happy New Year!"

The girl beamed; then she grabbed him and planted her red lips solidly on his, stepped back, rolling her blue eyes suggestively. Then she turned and was lost in a sea of people moving toward the dance floor.

Jim looked on, frowning. Then he pulled Sue with him toward the crowd.

Sarah stood and moved quickly toward the door. She did not look back. As the door closed behind her, she heard the crowd go crazy with excitement, counting out the last seconds of the old year.

And there was her cab waiting out front.

"Where to, lady?"

"Back to sanity," she said, and she drew in the first full breath of air she had taken all evening.

"I never heard of it," the cab driver said.

"Home," Sarah said. Then she gave him the address.

Plot, Character, and Setting

The setting is the ballroom, and the new year is rapidly approaching. Characterizations of several people emerge from the actions at the table and on the floor. The third person narrator switches from one character to another, much like a reporter at a political convention,but we are always aware that other characters are introduced to accent the conflict developing at the table between Sarah and Arnold and to provide the imagery and excitement of an approaching new year in the ballroom.

Who is the antagonist? We must interpret the actions of Sarah and those of Arnold before we make any decision about *who* or *what* is the major cause of the breakdown in the couple's relationship? Implications are clear that both have failed, since both have never learned to communicate their feelings.

This is Sarah's story, told in the third person, limited-omniscient point-of-view. Most of what we learn about the characters comes from their actions and their spoken words; however, Sarah's thoughts tell us even more. We see that both Arnold and Sarah are immature and irresponsible. She should have broken off the date before this situation could develop. This is no sudden decision on her part. Arnold, on the other hand, displays the same immaturity. He cannot be surprised when she walks out on him, just as everyone else is dancing to "Auld Lang Syne." Surely he has heard these cuts before, has heard them here at the party, and has ignored them.

Jim and Sue Penniweather and the waitress—the subordinate characters—are used to produce the New Year's incident in counterpoint. The mood is a contrasting one of excitement and frustration, of boredom and, on the part of Arnold, an awakening to a dreaded reality. The party atmosphere is both confusing and exciting as the forces of counterpoint merge to help unravel the plot and to help us visualize the setting.

Perhaps, however, the two are exhibiting a reaction to an earlier event. The situation here, then, would be crucial. Maybe Arnold is very intelligent, but Sarah happens to be one of those people who want to change others. If so, and Arnold does take off in hot pursuit, the plot could take off. Remember, this dialogue represents only one incident in the story. There will be several incidents before and after this one, each of these contributing to the plot. All these incidents will go toward completing your Sarah–Arnold episode. Obviously, then, plotting before you write is important.

Symbolic References

This writing sample didn't contain any symbols, but if it had, the drama would have become more significant. Suppose in an earlier incident we had planted "blue smoke rings" floating above the head of an "extra" who was sitting next to the young lovers on their first date. There's nothing unusual about seeing smoke rings, but let's make certain these are perfectly shaped, expanding, and not easily broken. Then on this night, Arnold becomes our smoke ring blower. These are perfect, too, until the waitress steps in and teasingly swats at them, destroying that perfection. Here, the second occurrence of the smoke rings is observed by Sarah, giving the initial observation its symbolic reference and meaning. The symbol is used to parallel a crisis in the plot. Perhaps she suspects Arnold of seeing another woman.

Dialogue: A Refreshing Change

Dialogue is a refreshing sight after long passages of narrative, as one often finds regularly in both genres of prose fiction. We enjoy hearing people speak for themselves; the story becomes easier to follow. Dialogue can actually turn us on to reading the stories.

Occasionally, we discover counterpoint in plotting incidents—where contrasting story elements converge and reinforce events—just as it sometimes occurs within the dialogue. You will find it worthwhile to keep counterpoint in mind as you examine other examples of dialogue in short stories and novels.

19

Developing Flashbacks

Writers don't always agree when it is appropriate to introduce the flashback. Some maintain that flashbacks can appear anywhere in the story—beginning, middle, or ending. Others are quick to warn us never to present a flashback close to the beginning, before we have established our protagonist with a real-to-life image in the present. How, then, can a beginner know when to use the flashback? Actually, you must first learn how to develop flashbacks that do what you want them to do. A serious analysis of several samples in short stories and novels will help you make the right decisions about the appropriate timing and purpose for your flashbacks and about the effectiveness of the transitions that make them work.

A Common Problem

Writers sometimes find themselves in an awkward plotting situation: The main character is called upon to exhibit a special skill or knowledge the writer has failed to mention earlier. Using a flashback in such instances can seem forced, thus failing to make the later actions more credible. One solution in such instances is to begin your story at an earlier point. You might simply supply an extra scene to reveal the knowledge or skills your protagonist will need to overcome some conflict, or to characterize an individual who must eventually accomplish outstanding feats. Experience, however, teaches us that carefully pre-plotting stories avoids unnecessary rewriting and flashbacks that do not improve the plot in some way.

Purposes for Flashbacks

Let's examine several other purposes for using flashbacks:

1. The flashback may be used to emphasize the seriousness of any situation, supplying information that intensifies the conflict and makes it appear unsolvable.

2. The flashback can cover several chapters, including a complete episode in the life of a protagonist. The background provided helps us identify with the character who must eventually face a formidable crisis.

3. The flashback may introduce another character and information that makes that character a worthy antagonist.

4. The flashback might shed new light upon a current problem, foreshadowing a new course of action, or hinting of impending disaster.

5. The flashback may include characterizations or details

that provide motivations for future actions by your principal characters.

6. The flashback may be an obligatory incident, used to help the reader tie loose ends of the plot together before the next crisis occurs.

Story Beginnings

The beginning of your story usually introduces your protagonist, who is involved in an absorbing situation. Bits of essential information are woven into the action to provide imagery and character. Any flashback should not be introduced before these images are clear to us, nor until we have some idea of the stuff your protagonist is made of.[1]

The flashback is more effective when the reader is engrossed in the scene and barely realizes that the story has shifted to past action until the writer brings him back to the present. Through descriptions of events that happened months or years ago, even earlier in the same day, readers get a clearer understanding of the present situation and of the characters involved.[2]

An Exception

Colleen McCullough's novel, *The Thornbirds,* introduces a flashback on the first page. Although it takes us into an earlier period in the life of her protagonist, the flashback is brief, well crafted, and hardly noticeable. This is the story of Meggie, drawn into an affair with Ralph, an Outback parish priest.

The novel begins in 1915, when Meggie has reached her fourth birthday. The breakfast dishes were washed and put away before her mother presented her with a brown paper parcel and ordered her outside. Meggie was as clumsy as any four-year-old when she excitedly attacked the heavy wrapping. Her excitement mounted as she caught familiar scents of the Wahine general store. She knew that whatever she uncovered in the package had been "store bought," not something homemade or maybe donated by someone who had no further use for it.

> "Agnes! Oh, Agnes!" she said lovingly, blinking at the doll lying there in a tattered nest.
>
> A miracle indeed. [And the flashback follows] Only once in her life had Meggie been into Wahine; all the way back in May, because she had been a very good girl.

The flashback continues to provide details of Meggie riding into town with her mother and seeing that beautiful doll seated on the store counter. The doll's dress was of pink satin with an abundance of cream lace frills. Before the glimpse into the past comes to a close, we have learned that Meggie has never owned a doll and has never realized that dolls and little girls go together. Surrounded by older brothers, she has played happily with their discards of whistles, slingshots, or toy soldiers.

Finally, we are brought back to the present, to Meggie seated outside the house, opening her package and uncovering the doll, Agnes. Note how the following sentence brings us smoothly back to that point:

> Stroking the bright pink folds of the dress, grander than any she had ever seen on a human woman, she picked Agnes up tenderly.

This flashback introduces characterizations of both Meggie and her mother. When we return to the present, we discover the character in each of her brothers. The brothers are quick to seize upon an opportunity to torment the four-year-old. They seize the doll from her grasp and toss it about, creating much distress for Meggie who is no match for them. Finally, an older brother, Frank, who is fifteen, steps in and frightens the younger pranksters away; however, the doll is left in disarray and Meggie is distraught.

Sometimes writers need a paragraph or two to take us from present to past action. In the short story, however, you cannot allow such long transitional passages, nor can you flashback so often that the story "ping-pongs," creating confusion rather than clarification. Again, the beginner must practice and polish his craft until the reader can be taken backwards in time and forward to the present without realizing what has been done.[3]

Novels Patterned with a Major Flashback

Earlier you learned that some novel patterns use a flashback that contains a major portion of the novel. The story opens at the beginning, and flashes back for several chapters before picking up the story again. James Leo Herlihy's novel, *Midnight Cowboy,* follows this pattern in Part One of the three-part novel. Chapter 1 introduces the protagonist as he is about to make the first big move in his life—he's about to take a Greyhound bus to the East where he intends to become a gigolo and earn some big money. The author then flashes back for the remaining chapters of Part One, giving us information about the kind of life the protagonist has experienced. By the time we get to Part Two, Joe Buck is "riding toward his destiny."[4]

The extensive flashback has supplied information that makes the reader feel a cautious, tongue-in-cheek response to Joe Buck's high expectations. The end is foreshadowed.

Backtracking with Exposition

Expositional narrative can explain what happened in the past, using a first or third person storyteller. The viewpoint character tells us what has already taken place. Though dialogues are often included, they must be essential. The purposes for expositional passages are similar to those of the flashback incident, but brevity and need are the guiding principles governing their usage. They may appear at any point of your story, short story or novel.

The following excerpt will demonstrate these points. This is a first person account from Ann Hood's "Fanning An Old Flame," *Redbook,* March 1989. The beginning introduces us to the protagonist, Winnie, who has invited "an old flame," Michael, to dinner. A fine meal should win any man's heart, she thinks, and she is determined to win Michael's. Michael comes to dinner, and the conversation uncovers a major crisis. He announces abruptly that he has fallen in love with a delightful English girl named Arabelle.

> "Winnie," he tells me, "she's beautiful."

She listens painfully as Michael recalls a number of interesting things about Arabelle. The girl has a delightful way of talking. "Bangs" are called "fringe." But Winnie is not amused.

> "Can you believe it?" he says, still chuckling. "Fringe."

Now the principal character takes us into a flashback, using a paragraph of expositional backtracking:

> I have known Michael for almost seven years. We met in college. Then he moved to Boston for law school and I moved to Cleveland. Then he moved to Cleveland and I moved to Boston. We just missed each other like that in city after city, for years. Sometimes one of us flew to visit the other for a weekend and we would marvel at how well we got along, how right we were for each other. But we would say, you live in Cleveland and I live in Boston. . . .

The exposition reveals Winnie's earlier lack of determination in capturing Michael's heart. Through the expositional backtracking, we learn that the meal is not enough to catch her man, for her past and present actions ignore some very important ingredients.

Moving with Transitions

A number of transitional devices are used in short stories and novels to move us smoothly into the flashback. Ann Hood's expositional passage prepares us for the brief look backwards with one transitional sentence:

> "I have known Michael for almost seven years."

Now let's examine several other devices: First, let's witness how a bird, music, shadows on the water, ripples in a pool, rain, the wind, or a special setting can open the door to the past.[5]

I was grateful when Corey, my husband of twelve wonderful years, volunteered to take our eleven-year-old son, Sean, for a weekend of camping and hiking at Paris Mountain State Park. The house I grew up in was to be put up for sale, and I needed to clean the place up before placing a sign in the front yard.

Saturday went by quickly. That night I settled down in my parent's bedroom, and the comforts of the feather mattress hastened the arrival of sleep.

The next morning, I was awakened early, aroused by the choruses of robins feeding upon the freshly seeded lawns. From the bedroom window I saw a blue jay fly in from the uncultivated fields beyond the fences and come to rest on a low fence post. He fidgeted and squawked his protests to the robins, and, when they seemed to ignore him, he made frantic efforts to dart in among them, pecking at them, hoping to drive them away.

Beyond the fences, the uncultivated fields stretched as far as the rich bottom land near the river. These were now overgrown with scrubby, blackjack oak, young pine saplings, and tall grasses. I saw the changes that time and the seasons had contributed to my surroundings. And I remembered another spring, six years earlier.

Now we are prepared to move backwards in time. The descriptions of the changing land and the final sentence have provided a smooth transition.

I saw Papa as he reached the gate opening into the yard behind the house. For a man in his late sixties, I knew the sun bore down hard upon him, and I grew more concerned about his heart.

"Why don't you stop working so hard, Papa?" I asked. "Come live with me, Corey, and your grandson."

His shirt had soaked through with sweat. He came upon the porch, drew a dipper of cool water from the pail I had filled from the well moments earlier. "Don't fuss with me, Laura. My body's a lot like that old tractor I just put away under the shed. If I don't work it, it'll grow rusty real fast."

I didn't argue with Papa. Experience had taught me to express what I felt, and when he decided I was right, he would let up a little.

Actually, he began to work less under the sun as spring grew closer to summer. I visited him more often when he began to complain of dizziness and shortness of breath. I kept pleading with him to come home with me so that I could take care of him. He said he'd think about it.

In April and May, rain was plentiful. Melon vines crept beyond the rows, intermingled, and spread a mass of leafy green cover, protecting the young melons and conserving moisture until soon they were very visible, growing large and plentiful by late June.

Then it was July. I was setting the breakfast table, when my father opened the screen door and stepped into the kitchen. "Right on time," he grinned.

I poured his coffee. He looked up at me and saw I was delighted. I thought he was referring to breakfast. Breakfast had always been ready by seven. I never forgot that schedule, even though I had been married for twelve years, helping to manage my own home and to keeping my own family together.

But I learned right away that I had not interpreted his statement correctly. "The melons," he added. "They're right on time."

Before I could say anything, we heard voices from the melon field. Papa was up and out of the house, and I was close behind him. Darting among the rows of ripe melons were three boys, none of them older than twelve. They couldn't have seen us, for they continued to scamper about, thumping the melons for ripeness.

Papa slipped past me and was back inside the house. I heard the pantry door close, and then he was back upon the porch, shouting a warning and waving a double-barreled shotgun. Seconds later, he fired both rounds into the air, but not before the youngsters had fled into the nearby woods with their melons.

Afterwards, I heard Papa chuckling with delight as he put the shotgun away. It suddenly dawned upon me what he had been referring to when he said, "Right on time." He had planted those melons to enjoy such moments that only those boys and the holidays would bring.

Now the transition brings us back to the present:

The old house is quiet now. Down below, the blue jay has given up his protest for the present and has flown away.

Transitions can also result from answering a question raised in the dialogue:

Mel stopped the truck at the rear of the house, in the shade of a great pecan tree. Jody got out and let his eyes travel over the building's exterior walls. The paint had cracked and peeled, but the foundation had held, and he observed how the walls and roof showed no signs of rot and sag.

Further investigations revealed that the barns and the corrals were empty. Jody felt his dream begin to fade.

"What happened?"

"A lot of changes took place after you left. Small farmers couldn't make it. I did what I could to help, and your father sent money regularly." Mel pulled a clump of sour grass, broke off a stem of it and chewed it. Spat it out.

"Consolidation," Jody said.

"Exactly. When things got real bad, I took your grandparents to live with me. We sold most of the land."

"The house?"

"Your grandfather said nothing must keep you from getting the house and barns."

Jody turned and started walking toward the car. "I want to see my grandparents, Uncle Mel."

"Don't you want to see inside the house?"

"It wouldn't be the same . . . not without them."

A number of additional questions could have been raised by either Jody or his uncle Mel, each answered with important details to explain the deterioration of the farm and the great framed house. The passage of time could have been filled in for us, as well. Still, this brief sample characterizes Jody, his uncle Mel, and the grandparents and provides an opening for a new episode in Jody's life.

The author might flashback and return to the present all in the same paragraph, providing very short transitions:

> I felt the exhilaration sweep over me, followed by a butterfly-light gutsy feeling, signaling something good was happening in our house. The red velvet case that had once held my brother's gold watch now lay open on the coffee table. My dad had given Frank that watch for Christmas, ten long years earlier. But if my current exhilaration was borne on the wings of hope, that earlier Christmas season had left our family split with little hope of reconciliation. The watch had been thrown aside in the heat of rebellion and anger. Voices rose to fever pitch, ending several minutes later when Frank came down the stairs with his bags packed, pushing aside my mother's tearful attempts to restrain him, while my dad just as heatedly lashed

> out at him, driving him on, until Frank had left the house, slamming the door in one last gesture of rebellion. And who could remember just how it all started? But the ending—you felt the pain of it long afterwards, through the cold winter days with their recurrent snows maintaining a sheet of white cover over the earth. But the deepest pain kept returning when I recalled the sounds of anger and the slamming of the door behind my brother. Then there was that terrible silence that fell upon our house when it was obvious my brother would not return. Until now, and I felt the rising hope as soon as I spotted the red velvet watchcase lying open on the coffee table. And then there were voices upstairs. Even before I heard the footfalls on the stairs, I knew Frank had come home again. . . .

What transitional sentence leads us into the flashback? "The red velvet case that had once held my brother's gold watch now lay open upon the coffee table." Now the flashback begins: "My dad had given Frank that watch for Christmas, ten long years earlier." Then we are brought back to the present: "Until now, and I felt the rising hope as soon as I spotted the red velvet watchcase lying open on the coffee table."

Read in an unbroken sequence of a single paragraph, reader emotions are drawn from the present into the past and back again in a rapid flow of related, supportive details.

20

Developing a Narrative Hook

We enjoy stories that stimulate strong feelings about characters and situations that are about familiar settings, and that contain changing moods and believable actions in each plot sequence. We want to become absorbed in the conflict, identifying with the story people and pulling for them to succeed. We want to become readers who care.

Our caring does not happen by accident. You have already learned how writers often use several plot elements to capture interests and to nourish each incident so that it becomes real for us. We have seen how the magic of symbols, foreshadowings, flashbacks, and dialogues can bring colors, shapes, time, actions, and emotions to life. But there is an additional writing tool not previously mentioned here that, in the short story at least, appears more often than symbols—the narrative hook.

This strong narrative statement in the first or second paragraph of a story hooks us with immediate significance and is referred to repeatedly as the plot develops. This statement, planned before you actually write your story, helps readers stay in step with the action and experience a greater comprehension of conflict, theme, and plot. This unifying device should be placed in the first one hundred words of your story, the sooner the better, and may be a single sentence or a paragraph.

Recognizing Narrative Hooks

Marjorie Franco, *Redbook*'s most published author—*Redbook* has published forty-two of her stories as of the time of this writing—has skillfully planted a narrative hook in the first paragraph of "Chance of A Lifetime," *Redbook,* March 1989. Let's examine the hook and determine how she uses it to unify the plot, to accent the conflict, to characterize our protagonist, and to throw light upon the theme.

> It was the stranger at the door, early that morning who got Conrad to thinking about his life. The man was middle-aged and clean-cut; he had dark hair, a strong, tanned face, and he wore an expensive gray suit. He reminded Conrad of Molly's father, but unlike Molly's father, this man treated him with respect.

A professional writer learns how to get the reader interested early, at the beginning of the story. How has this author done this?

1. The protagonist and antagonist are identified in the opening paragraphs. Conrad is our protagonist. The stranger at the door is a minor character who plays a significant part in reawakening an old, unpleasant experience with his father-

in-law: "It was the stranger at the door, early that morning who got Conrad thinking about his life."

2. The narrative hook is introduced as the last sentence of the opening paragraph: "He reminded Conrad of Molly's father, but unlike Molly's father, this man treated him with respect." We have been introduced to our antagonist, Molly's father. Though the man remains in the background, his words become a voice that haunts the couple for too long. Read that statement again. It will be used again and again to deliver the psychological impact upon Conrad and Molly. It will become the driving force that motivates both these characters to work especially hard to become a success.

Plotting the Hook

The narrative hook does not leap out and identify itself when it first appears in the opening paragraph. Actually, it is little more than a seed that has been planted, to be nourished at key intervals as the plot unravels. What Conrad's father-in-law thinks of him is the seed for generating and sustaining conflict. After you have read the story and are reflecting on it, the recurrences of the narrative statement will stand out sharply.

Molly feels and thinks much more than the author is ready for us to know in the beginning. But if these thoughts and feelings were revealed in the early parts of the story, the effect would be disastrous. What the author decides not to tell us becomes the powerful truth brought to light in the climax. The uncovering of the truth lends emotional impact to the conclusion and gives us our theme.

At this point, we have been introduced to a stranger, and can guess that his presence will lead us almost immediately into the conflict. The first sentence gives us a clue about what the major concern of the plot will be: Conrad's past experiences, uncovered in present and past actions, reveal very strong motives for him to get the antagonist (his father-in-law) to think differently of him. Anxiety and confusion set in as Conrad examines his past and considers the stranger's offer. At every key turn, our antagonist emerges ever present in Conrad's mind, though he does not appear in the present. All references to him are in the flashbacks and in the repetitions of the narrative statement.

After presenting her protagonist and planting the narrative hook, we learn why the stranger has come to the farm. The subordinate character's purpose is to present the "chance of a lifetime." The stranger is allowed to look over the property. He tells them how pleased he is with the commercial improvements Molly has made by adding a tea room, as well as Conrad's conversion of the barn, turning it into an antique shop. Conrad watches the man, feeling a sense of pride in his own and Molly's accomplishments.

At this point, the seed planted earlier reappears as a full-blown minor crisis. We again see Conrad's deep, driving motive when the hook appears for a second time in a flashback:

> When they were first married, Conrad and Molly had lived in town, struggling under the prophecy of failure, set down by Molly's father, who had declared Conrad a loser.

Another brief flashback details the couple's hard work in making changes when the farm became a losing business. Again the hook appears, as well as a premise upon which we will construct a statement of the theme:

> Inheriting the farm had changed their lives, given them a new start, a chance to prove themselves, if not to Molly's father, then at least to each other.

We learn that Conrad spent much of his childhood following his grandfather around the farm. The work had been difficult, but he treasured the experiences it afforded him. We are then brought back to the present when the stranger asks whether Conrad was raised on the farm. No, he wasn't. He had grown up in town. When his grandfather died, he left the farm to Conrad.

Finally, the stranger writes out a check for the purchase of the farm, and Conrad stuffs it into his pocket without looking at it. This move clues us to the battle raging in Conrad's mind. Molly is present, and he is trying to decide what she wants, for he recalls how hard she has worked to make the farm a paying enterprise.

Then Molly asks, "Aren't you going to look at it?"

He does. The offer is for a very large sum. He gets the uneasy feeling that she really wants to sell.

And the narrative hook follows:

> The chance of a lifetime. . . . Most important, he could show Molly's father that he wasn't a loser after all; he could command his respect as a person of means.

The characterizations of both Conrad and Molly clearly indicate a major flaw in their behaviors, one that lets their problem mushroom until it's about to burst. They are not able to communicate their true feelings. Obviously, Molly isn't helping matters either. She's just as undecided about selling as Conrad is.

Conrad begins to have doubts about himself. What kind of man is he?

> Would he sacrifice the farm and what he and Molly had accomplished in order to convince her father to think well of him?

Now he is convinced Molly wants to sell the place, but the communication between them is poor, aggravating the situation. In the next plot incident, we are drawn into reminiscences about how Conrad found and purchased antiques for his shop, and further reminiscences surrounding his traditional farm duties. Then he makes his decision to sell. He's certain that's what Molly wants.

When Conrad makes the decision to sell, the emotional strings are ready to snap. Voices reach fever pitch one evening when Conrad returns from an auction sale. Finally, Molly communicates her true feelings about the farm. She tells Conrad that she loves the farm and her life as it is. She has only gone along with his idea of selling the farm because she knows he wants to prove himself to her father.

Her statement frees him from the need to prove himself to her father. Molly's words let him know how pleased she is with him and with the life they have made together. The strings pulling upon their emotions relax as both manage to communicate their true feelings.

The Theme

Conrad poses the question: "Was it better to be a loser in another man's eyes than to be a loser in one's own?" Molly's words help Conrad find the answer: It is better to be a loser in another man's eyes than to be a loser in one's own.

Conrad wants to give Molly everything she wants; yet, he moved intuitively rather than first making an effort to find out what she really thinks about important things. This flaw, the stranger who offers them the chance of a lifetime, and the narrative statement make up the three volatile forces in conflict, until common sense cries out above high-strung voices: "Communicate!"

The hook is indelibly printed in our minds, providing conflict until the very end when Molly erases its hold over them with a few simple words of love and appreciation. Her feelings have been withheld from us in the beginning and unleashed at the end to create the effect the author wants to close with. We have an ending that presents satisfaction and calm resolution.

A Second Look

We have now seen how writers hook their readers and keep them hooked with a narrative statement laid very early in the plot. In the next example, let's begin our analyses by reflecting on what we have learned to expect from a narrative hook. If our expectations are met in the second example, then our analysis of the effect of the narrative hook in the first example is a practical one. Thus reassured, we can feel justified in using this technique again and again in writing stories that will hook our readers.

Our second example, "The Restless Ones," written by Leslie Waller, concerns a seventeen-year-old adolescent, named Jerry who finds himself bored and restless. Our antagonist is clearly the flaw-ridden conscience of the adolescent, introduced in the opening of the story as Jerry lies in bed, feigning an illness and dodging his problems, and in the flashbacks that reveal the adolescent behaviors of his friends.

Those friends, like himself, have reached the brink of maturity with a very serious problem pressing upon them. His fantasies emerge and smother the reality of his actions and those of his adolescent friends.

The narrative statement appears as the first sentence of the story:

> They wouldn't electrocute somebody my age, Jerry thought.

What follows is a detailed description of what he hears going on downstairs, as the rest of the family goes on with the business of living. But Jerry is suffering. Failing to discuss his problem, it looms larger, and he imagines himself going through the stages of trial and punishment for the crime he and his friends have committed.

The fourth paragraph emphasizes the hook:

> He grimaced and turned on his side, looking at the faint line of light under his closed door. You got the electric chair, he decided, for first-degree murder. But what was it for second-degree? Or for manslaughter? A life sentence, probably.

Each flashback reveals what the restless youths do to bring excitement into their lives. Here we learn of the crime that has taken place during a moment of such restlessness. These antics show us the importance teenagers give to action in their daily lives, a sharp contrast to the mature individual who is satisfied with contemplating his goals and learning successful ways to achieve them.

Jerry's actions are destructive. His thoughts and reactions are layered with fantasy, and he is unable to communicate with his family about what he has done. A character flaw is uncovered in his adolescent behavior. We discover Jerry's inadequacy as he reviews what he has done and fantasizes about what should and will undoubtedly happen to him.

The conclusion becomes clear and credible to us when we see the youngster come face to face with the reality of his crime. He weeps.

> Ashamed, he wiped his wet face with the back of his hand.
>
> The juvenile officer spoke to him: "Sometimes . . . it's good to cry."
>
> "It's kid stuff," Jerry said.
>
> "No," the man replied. "Not any more it isn't. Not when you've grown up."

From Theory to Application

Not all stories have narrative hooks, and those that do have them aren't always as clearly structured as the ones studied in this chapter. Even in those stories that use this technique, the strings of emotion are not pulled with full force all at once, but we feel them tightening more as our protagonist is identified as a real human being or a human element creates a problem. Perhaps, as the plot unfolds, an additional burden of human frailty makes us identify with even more of the pain.

Before working in a narrative hook, your plot should be clear in your head and your characters clearly delineated in your mind and in descriptive sketches on paper. Determine what important information must be withheld from the reader until the end? What flaws in your protagonist will help you plan each incident so that the tensions mount until the flaws are corrected or overcome? After these decisions are made, you are ready to write your opening paragraphs, planting a statement or two as guiding hooks to draw and retain readers' interest up to the end. The narrative hook will serve as a catalyst for plotting each situation that follows. It will tie each incident together, forward or in flashbacks, culminating in a tightly organized and satisfying plot.

21

Three Power Techniques: Imagery, Pace, and Transitions

The style of writing you present to your audience will be largely governed by your education. Composition skills are critical elements of style, learned and developed in your speech and writing since you first began putting your thoughts on paper. Still, you may know everything there is to know about words, sentence structures, paragraph development, outlining an essay, or plotting a short story and still be unable to write with an interesting, readable style. *Style* is learned through experience. *Composition* is taught first, and, through writing and speaking experiences, the individual elements of composition become the natural but essential ingredients of an effective style.

Three Magic Ingredients

To list and give examples of each element of composition would require a separate handbook. Composition and grammar texts and a number of handbooks on the subject are readily available, so we will give attention here to only *three effective elements* that help writers present their ideas in an enviable manner. These three elements have the most immediate effect upon your writing style: (1) imagery drawn from a selective sensory vocabulary and a variety of sentence formations; (2) pace; and (3) transitional devices.

Developing a Sensory Vocabulary

One of the earliest signs of a potential writer is a genuine interest in words. We hear words on radio, or see and hear them on television. We spot interesting words in print. We catch words in lectures and conversations and make notes of these. At the first opportunity, we use these words to lend authority and impact to our discussions and our writing. Readers and listeners of our work are quick to recognize the strong imagery and sensory perceptions evident in our unique selections of words and in our variety of sentence formations.

Imagery

Supplying imagery—those picture-forming descriptions that increase reader perception—involves a careful selection of concrete nouns, purposeful adjectives, essential adverbs, and power verbs that help the reader form sharp visualizations of characters, setting, action, and mood. In addition, *figurative language* is a powerful tool that lends force, clarity, and beauty to your passages. As with other element of style, this imagery working must be examined in the works of professional writers and practiced with devotion to assure your success with it. Readers are able to imagine a lot of things, but you still have to provide essential details to awaken and sharpen their perceptions.

Let's examine an excerpt from an O. Henry contribution, "The Princess and the Puma," to determine how imagery can be achieved:

> There was a fine waterhole in the riverbed. The banks were thickly covered with great trees, undergrown with brush. Back from the waterhole fifty yards was a stretch of curly mesquite grass—supper for his horse and bed for himself. Givens staked his horse and spread out his saddle blankets to dry.
>
> He sat down with his back against a tree and rolled a cigarette. From somewhere in the dense timber along the river came a sudden, rageful shivering wail. The pony danced at the end of his rope and blew a whistling snort of a comprehending fear. Givens puffed at his cigarette, but he reached leisurely for his pistol-belt, which lay on the grass, and twirled the cylinder of his weapon tentatively. A great gar plunged with a loud splash into the waterhole. A little brown rabbit skipped around a bunch of catclaw and sat looking humorously at Givens. The pony went on eating grass. (O. Henry, "The Princess and the Puma," 1907)

Here we have a clear, rhythmic style that we can read aloud easily. We do not stumble over uneven, tongue-tripping phrases. Images are quickly drawn from several power verbs, and a selection of modifiers sharpen the perceptions gotten from both verbs and nouns.

Note that all sentences do not open with the subjects up front. The variety in sentence openers give the passage a transitional flow of action and mood in a setting that is easy for us to visualize: (1) "Back from the waterhole fifty yards," and (2) "From somewhere in the dense timber along the river." These openers provide spatial directions, helping us to follow the action.

Nine Ways to Open a Sentence

Using a *variety of sentence openers* adds sparkle to your writing style. Not only do they assist you in developing smooth transitions of time, space, and importance, but they also help break the monotony of repeated, subject-first sentence formations.

1. Use a prepositional phrase.
   Out of the black, mushrooming cloud, a great bolt of white lightning charged the atmosphere with ominous, jagged streaks of frightening intensity.

2. Use an infinitive or an infinitive phrase.
   To swim was his purpose for going to the lake.
   To ship the goods early, he would first have to secure the goods and label them properly.
   To ship the goods early was critical for his success. (Infinitive phrase as the subject.)

3. Use a verb.
   Give this lesson your best efforts.

4. Use a gerund or a gerund phrase.
   Reading is often rewarding.
   Knowing your subject requires a careful attention to details.

5. Use an adverb.
   Yesterday, the science class ventured into the fields for on-site studies of flora and fauna.

6. Use an adverbial clause.

When we complete the rough draft of the chapter, let us think of revisions that will improve it.

7. Use an expletive.
   Well, why not look at other alternatives for your solution?

8. Use a noun clause.
   Whatever John does is usually done well.
   Whomever he names will be chosen by the party.
   Whoever reaches the finish line first will be declared the winner.
   Who won the race will be announced today.
   Whom they finally select will receive the Grand Prize.

9. Ask a question.
   How may we contribute to your success?
   What does the evidence reveal to us?

You won't want to use all of these openers in a few paragraphs. Too many of them used in a short span produces work that is contrived. At first, your main concern is learning to use a variety of openers and a variety of structures. As you practice writing, let your thoughts draw upon those sentence formations that are fitting for the moment. During your revisions, you may decide to eliminate or add other openers to get the results you need. A great deal of thought and writing practice is essential, especially for beginners.

What Openers Tell Us

Transitional openers can tell us a lot: They might give us the spatial directions we need to follow the action within the setting; they might provide us with details of the time consumed during the scene; and they might provide us with the order of the details in an incident.

Notice how these openers become space transitions:

1. Three feet in front of him,
2. A foot above his head,
3. Hundreds of feet below,

Notice how these openers provide time order transitions:

1. Immediately,
2. Twenty seconds later,
3. Then,

Notice how these openers provide order of importance:

1. First, John studied the pamphlet carefully.
2. Then, while the students waited anxiously,
3. Finally,

Direct Transitions

Direct transitions affect the flow of ideas within sentences, between sentences, and between paragraphs. The sentence openers presented above are considered to be direct transitions. In addition to these openers, a number of connectives is also considered to be direct transitions. These connectives link the thought of two clauses.

Direct transitional connectives and their thought relationships:

1. In New York, almost a million people picked him to become their governor; *however*, over a million others voted for the winning candidate. (contrast)

2. Evelyn volunteered to do the clerical work, *and* Sue offered to write the promotional materials. (same line of thought)

3. Either you will study and practice, *or* you will not succeed. (correlation)

4. Nobody had prepared for the assignment; *therefore*, the professor offered a lecture on the subject. (consequence or inference)

5. The primary high school text became inadequate, *for* most students had already advanced several stages beyond its instructional content. (reason)

6. John and Ellen were unable to collect the needed funds to save their farm; *nor* were they able to finance their eldest daughter's education. (alteration or choice)

Indirect Transitions

Indirect transitions are achieved in two ways: (1) The author can replace a key word with another; and (2) the author can emphasize a word or phrase by repeating it several times in the paragraph or longer theme.

(1)

The President of Chile was ousted in an orderly November coup. In spite of his having been exiled to Peru, this great humanitarian is revered by millions of Chileans for his noble efforts to ease the ravages of hunger, corruption and disease, long rampant among two-thirds of that country's people. A man of vision, Burinda labored tirelessly, unselfishly, in his quests for democratic reforms. Yet, these concerns for his countrymen alarmed the ambitious generals who immediately toppled the statesman and established a military dictatorship.

Key words:	Replacements:
president	humanitarian, man of vision, Burinda, statesman
Chile	country
people	Chileans, countrymen
ousted	exiled, toppled
generals	military dictatorship

(2)

Our enemies are supporting the wrong measures for our needed social, political and economic reforms. Our enemies are using criminal tactics to undermine our progressive, democratic efforts to remedy current situations, while failing to offer any solutions that will stabilize our government. Our enemies will not be successful. When the time is ripe, our harvest shall mean a return to peace and prosperity. We will win this struggle for the benefit of all our people. We will win because we are right.

Repetition: Our enemies (three times)
We will win (twice)

Pace: Action Verbs and Verbals

The following excerpt from *The Last Convertible,* by Anton Myrer, is an impressive illustration of how effective a selective vocabuary can become. As the battle gets underway, note how the pace of the action is accented and accelerated by the uses of verbs, verbals, effective phrasings, and varying sentence lengths. Other devices mentioned in this chapter are also present. Can you recognize them?

> The blast of the M1 shocked me. Opp, firing, his whole body lifting and dropping with the recoil. An ejected shell struck me on the cheek, a sting I never felt. In a trance, bound in Duchemin's harsh command I raised the rifle, aimed it wobbling and dipping at the swelling, jostling cluster of figures, squeezed the trigger. Nothing happened. I was flooded instantly with the panic—all at once remembered the safety, pushed it off again. Too high. I'd fired too high. But with the gun's kick I was all right. The panicky trembling was all gone. I was calm as calm now. I emptied the clip, inserted another swiftly, aimed at a tall figure rushing near, dangerously near, his mouth gaped wide, distended. I fired, the man leaped upward twisting, his back arched fantastically, and fell away out of sight. Only a few now, dancing, bobbing: three, then one. Then none at all. Over on the left they were running back toward the woods and I tracked them, glad of the jarring, comforting kick of the rifle, seeking it. Now there was nothing but shadows that swayed and slid under the slipping, dying flare. (Anton Myrer, *The Last Convertible,* 1978, with the permission of the publisher)

This excerpt has all the magic elements: imagery, transition, and good pacing. Note the effects the verbs, verbals, and elliptical phrasings have upon the setting and the action. They provide sensory details that help us perceive the anxiety, tension, fear, and horror enacted on the battlefield.

Also, did you note the variety in sentence openers? and the transitional phrases within the sentences? "Over on the left," and "all at once," and "now there was nothing." Sharp details have been woven into the action, directing us so that we can follow and sense all that the writer wanted us to.

Phrasings for Pace and Emotion

Stephen King is recognized as one of the most, if not the most, popular weavers of horror and suspense tales. While the preceding passage illustrated the uses of effective words, phrases, and sentences to lend realism to the actions on the battlefield, King's excerpt, drawn from his novel, *Pet Sematery,* takes us several steps further. This excerpt is an account of the accidental death of Gage, Louis Creed's young son. We are made to sense the horror and to share the trauma of the incident. Read the passage several times. Determine what devices King uses to achieve this effect.

Steve Masterston, a physician's assistant at the hospital where Dr. Creed practices, is with Louis when the doctor recalls the incident in a flashback:

> . . . in his mind he saw Gage running across the lawn toward the road. They were yelling at Gage to come back, but he wouldn't—lately the game had been to run away from Mommy-Daddy—and they were chasing him, Louis quickly outdistancing Rachel, but Gage was running away from Daddy—that was the game—and Louis was closing the distance but too slowly, Gage was running down the mild slope of the lawn now to the verge of Route 15, and Louis prayed to God that Gage would fall down because a person's control over his legs didn't get really cool until he was maybe seven or eight. Louis prayed to God that Gage would fall down, fall down, yes, fall down bloody his nose crack his skull need stitches whatever, because now he could hear the drone of a truck coming toward

> them, one of those big ten wheelers that went back and forth endlessly between Bangor and the Orinco plant in Bucksport, and he had screamed Gage's name then, and he believed that Gage had heard him and tried to stop. Gage seemed to realize that the game was over, that your parents didn't scream at you when it was just a game, and he had tried to put on the brakes, and by then the sound of the truck was very loud, the sound of it filled the world. It was thundering. Louis had thrown himself forward in a long flying tackle, his shadow tracking the ground beneath him as the shadow of the Vulture had tracked the white late-winter grass of Mrs. Vinton's field that day in March, and he believed the tips of his fingers had actually brushed the back of the light jacket Gage had been wearing, and then Gage's forward motion had carried him out into the road, and the truck had been thunder, the truck had been sunlight on high chrome, the truck had been the deep-throated shrieking bellow of an air horn, that had been Saturday, that had been three days ago. (Stephen King, *Pet Sematery,* 1989, with the permissions of the publisher and author)

The rapid-fire phrasings draw us into the horrible incident and keep us there as the drama unfolds quickly. We identify with Louis and his efforts to pull his son from the hands of death. Sensory details again ensure dramatic, keenly focused visual and emotional imagery. Our protagonist becomes a strong figure; yet his strength is no match for the agonizing distance separating him from his son and the oncoming ten wheeler.

The punctuation is unique and purposeful. Unusual omissions cause us to feel some of the developing trauma, the rising hysteria, and the helplessness that leave Louis breathless, tense, and fearful. Through select, uninterrupted phrasings, our perceptions of the action and the setting are intensified. Note the choices of nouns, the uses of metaphor: "The truck had been sunlight on high chrome"; "the truck had been thunder"; and "the truck had been the deep-throated shrieking bellow of an air horn."

Transitions Between Scenes

How does the writer end one scene and move us into the next without causing confusion for the reader? Obviously, transitional devices are essential at these points, too. Here are several that you may have observed in stories you've read:

1. Use a blank space or indicate the time at the end of the first scene and at the beginning of the next. In an earlier chapter smooth transition was effected between two scenes—the taxi stand and the airport—through the use of this technique. The text clearly indicated that fifteen minutes elapsed between the two scenes.[1]

2. Use a person, place, thing or idea as a point for embarking upon the next incident.[2]

> The telephone rang. Garrett sat up. Stumbled over his new brown Oxfords as he grabbed the receiver. "Yes?"
>
> "What happened? You're late already."
>
> "Overslept, Mavis. Sorry. I won't be long."
>
> "That's the International Customs House. Next to City Transport. Got it?"
>
> "Got it."
>
> The shoes were too tight. The new leather squeaked, embarrassing him as he maneuvered past the people already assembled in the Customs House lobby.

3. Use dialogue to help readers anticipate the next scene.[3]

"You'll leave for boot camp tomorrow," the corporal explained. "You'll load on buses stationed on the blacktop at sunrise. You will be taken to the railway terminal in Columbia where you will board a special train that will take you to Ft. Gordon, Georgia. Dismissed!"

Ft. Gordon, Georgia was bristling with activity, when Joey disembarked from the train. In the distance, the youth heard the sounds of troops marching along the roads and singing in cadence.

4. Use an emotional link.[4]

Del finished his breakfast and sat back from the table. Glanced at the green floor tiles, saw them waver. He grabbed the glass of water and gulped down several swallows.

Don't panic, he tried to tell himself, even as he felt the pulling sensation in his left eye. He was certain the eyeball had moved in its socket, first toward the left and then to the right. He blinked his eye several times. Rubbed it. The movement stopped, but he felt a tightness and remained unsettled.

A tumor? Did he have a tumor?

Dr. Raymond Geller remained calm during his examination of Del. Finally, he looked up from the data he had assembled. "You don't have a tumor, Joey. Nerves . . . eye strain, perhaps."

5. When a scene ends and the next scene involves a new viewpoint character, tie the scenes together using transitional details or action.[5] Changing viewpoints in a short story is discouraged, but there will be times when the method will work best. Such changes occur regularly in novels of multiple viewpoints. To avoid confusion, make certain each

viewpoint character is a full, wholly visible figure before allowing another character—who must also be fully visible—to take over as the storyteller; the additional viewpoint character must be essential for telling the story.

> Jim followed Victor Schuyler's trail to the boathouse at Little Bear Landing. Yellow slits of light poured out through cracks in the walls. Then a shadow doused the light for a second or two. Jim drew up closer to the entrance.
>
> Victor Schuyler stepped back, glared at the boy who now sat bound and gagged in a corner. "You're stupid, boy! Stupid!" He turned toward another youth, his accomplice. "Take a look outside. He may not have followed alone."

Other equally satisfying methods will move your plots forward with an ease and pace that keep us interested.

22

Style: How Writers Express Themselves

A writer's style is his manner of expressing himself. When ideas are allowed to flow forth freely, results on paper will appear natural and unstilted, a work readers can tackle comfortably. When the natural flow of thoughts is interrupted for crafting and reshaping, there is always a danger of adding excessive description or burdensome details. A vivid example of such burdensome details is immediately recognizable in the work of James Fenimore Cooper, a popular American author of the nineteenth century.

James Fenimore Cooper

Before we examine Cooper's style, let's look into his background and learn something of the man, his education, and his accomplishments.

Cooper was born in Burlington, New Jersey, in 1789, the son of a politician who later became a judge. Tutored at home until he was fourteen, he entered Yale. After two years, he was expelled because of high-spirited behavior, and his father sent him to sea. While Cooper was away, his father was killed by a political opponent, and Cooper inherited a large estate. Soon afterwards, he married a woman who was instrumental in turning his attention to writing. His most successful novel was *The Spy,* often called the "first living American novel." Cooper created the forerunners of the westerns that became popular in the twentieth century. His pioneer novels are: *The Deerslayer, The Last of the Mohicans,* and *The Prairie*. He also wrote a number of seafaring adventures.[1] The following excerpt was taken from one of the latter tales, *The Pilot*.

(Barnstable, commander aboard the Ariel, has turned to his cockswain, Master Coffin, after sighting an enemy vessel.)

"Now I would wager a quintel of codfish, Master Coffin," said Barnstable, "against the best cask of porter that was ever brewed in England, that fellow believes a Yankee schooner can fly in the wind's eye! If he wishes to speak to us, why don't he give his cutter a little sheet, and come down?"

The cockswain had made his arrangements for combat, with much more method and philosophy than any other man in the vessel. When the drum beat to quarters, he threw aside his jacket, vest, and shirt, with as little hesitation as if he stood under an American sun, and with all the discretion of a man engaged in an understanding that required the free use of his utmost powers. As he was known to be a privileged individual in the Ariel, and whose opinions, in all matters of seamanship, were regarded as oracles by the crew, were listened to by his commander with no little demonstration of respect, the question excited no surprise. He was standing at the breach of his long gun, with his brawny arms folded on a breast that had been

> turned to the color of blood by long exposure, his grizzled looks fluttering in the breeze, and his tall form towering far above the heads of all near him.

When we read these passages aloud, we are able to do so with ease. Though the sentences are long and cluttered with descriptions that slow the pace of the action, the words flow quite evenly. Nevertheless, we are very annoyed by having to read over masses of descriptions when we have just been told an enemy vessel has been sighted. We want the action to get underway; we want reactions from the crew and additional details about the enemy that foreshadow worse difficulties ahead.

Cooper's descriptive atmosphere is too concentrated. Today, writers blend characterizations and atmosphere in palatable doses. Action scenes are described in short sentences with power verbs that create vivid mental pictures. Cooper's cluttered sentences delay the engagement, often making readers go back and reread passages to pick up the last important action. If you examine the entire novel, you will find descriptive clutter hamstringing much of the action throughout.

The critics of Cooper's day were not greatly influenced by how well his novels sold. They deplored the repetitious descriptions, his theatrical language, and his poor style. Yet, his readership grew. Cooper created American romantic pioneer stories that were almost contagious to readers of his times.[2]

An Effective Style

Good writing style emerges even when we make no real effort to create style; and, actually, style isn't something we want necessarily to concentrate on. Our first concern should be getting readers into our stories to feel the same excitement we feel while developing them.

Writers begin writing just as they learned to talk—naturally. But writing improves when you realize that writing is a lot like talking on paper. The difference is that you must draft and shape your writing to make your points clear to your readers, whereas in conversations you can supplement your words with body language and vocal inflections. We slip into grammatical lapses far more often in conversation than we do in print. Shaping the words as you put them down on paper inherently produces a style that is a shade more formal than we find in our conversations.[3]

Implications from Style

Through an author's style, a number of implications arise. Character, background, education, and personality are just a few of the key influences upon your writing style. Each of these provides us with clues to a writer's tastes, experiences, and feelings.

Though some elements of an author's style are obvious, writers don't plan it that way. Their writing style flows naturally from their experiences with thinking, timing, and what they feel about their stories. The lengths of paragraphs, word choices, varying lengths of sentences, and other developmental devices of composition are chosen subconsciously, given the writer's educational background; any rhythmic arrangement and resultant emotion stem from years of creative writing practice.

The most effective style is easy to read aloud. The sound of the reader's voice improves upon what we see on the printed page. For this reason, writers might read their stories aloud into the microphone and play it back to hear any tongue twisters that escaped them. The practice gives them an opportunity to try a variety of vocal inflections and to experience a combination of look and feel for rhythms and for an arrangement of thoughts that make the reading easier.

Style is not something that is taught; it is learned only through the writing process itself. Jesse Stuart was not certain how Mrs. Hatton, his high school English teacher, knew so much about style; the teacher had never written anything that he knew about. But she had taught school all her life and became a major inspiration for him. Stuart tells us that Mrs. Hatton believed that "thought came first and one developed a writing style through much practice putting his thoughts on paper."[4] She was quick to warn, "One shouldn't just try to do a style for style's sake."[5]

Style, then, must come naturally. How clever we become in choosing words does not make style any more than a man's or woman's hairdo defines personality. We uncover style only within the words. Writers must look for simple descriptions, dropping adjectives that do nothing more than add to a sentence's length.[6]

Writers read a lot. They check the titles on the best seller lists and find novels by other writers who would not be considered polished writers by most critics. Lawrence Block, columnist for *Writer's Digest* and author of about a hundred novels and books about writing, was reminded of a half dozen published writers whose opening chapters did not effectively maintain his interest. As a writer, he agreed that he was perhaps overly conscious of style and often found mechanical dialogues, awkward transitions, clumsy scene constructions and imprecise descriptions. Block decided that if he could make himself hang on for thirty or more pages, he would lose his excessive awareness of style and begin to perceive what was actually occurring in the plot.[7]

Obviously, Block is not saying it is okay to use mechanical dialogues and awkward transitions; as a successful writer, his keen eye can spot these flaws which damage the professional credibility of the author. The beginning writer is encouraged to write and rewrite until his manuscript is free of such flaws.

Evaluating Style

What does the story analyst look for in evaluating style? Here are five characteristics of an effective writing style:

1. Readability—Is the writing easy to read? Can you read it aloud without tripping over the words?

2. Action with forward movement (pace)—Do the events sustain the interest of the reader? Does the organization assure ease in comprehending what is happening at all times? Is the pace suitable for the action and the plot?

3. A writer's feel and excitement for his story—Jesse Stuart must have listened to his teacher. Readers of his realistic short stories and novels attest to their simple, straightforward style, to their warmth of feeling, and to their rich blend of human interest and compassion.

4. Discretion—The writer's discretion (or the lack of it) along with the subjects treated give us information about the writer's personality and interests; further, his manner of treatment tells us of his morality. In addition to these characteristics, we can uncover further information from the evidence he chooses to support his theme. Propaganda and

satirical novels are especially indicative of strong moral and intellectual qualities. Add some clever, imaginative fantasy, and we learn the author is highly creative and industrious.[8]

5. The writer's knowledge and experience—Knowledge of his subject, comprehension of the genre's development, and skill in presenting details in an orderly, exciting manner are expected of a professional writer.

Triumph Over Style

Many popular mainstream novels—those epic novels rendering in fictional form the great events that shaped a nation's history—amass great quantities of information for the reader. These books triumph over style because of the grandeur of their subject matter and the scope of their coverage. Leon Uris's *Exodus,* and Arthur Hailey's books illustrate such novels. This does not mean that these authors of great epic novels are clumsy stylists; however, it does emphasize that style in the great epic novels does not hold the same vital consideration as it does in shorter fiction.[9]

Hawthorne and Cooper: A Study in Contrasts

When we compare the background and writing style of Nathaniel Hawthorne, also a nineteenth-century writer, with that of Cooper, we uncover sharp contrasts in their backgrounds and styles.

Hawthorne was born in Salem, Massachussetts, scene of the infamous witchcraft trials that reached their heyday around 1692. The division caused by shame over the persecutions of innocent people must have lingered and haunted many a Puritan heart for many years thereafter. Hawthorne, over one hundred years later, examines the Puritan under the pressures of sin. His style is affected by his Puritan background, his personal identification with his story people, and his broad reading experience; his mother had encouraged him to put adventure aside and to become engrossed in books. From his knowledge and feelings about the changing standards of the world, he became especially concerned about the world's unchanging value system. He examined the Puritan community, revealing the lives of miserable souls who had sinned. At the same time, the reader is aware of Hawthorne's identification with these miserable souls.[10]

How does Hawthorne accomplish this dichotomy? A good example may be found in his characterization of Hester Prynne in *The Scarlet Letter*. He is critical of Puritan society; yet, he avoids overgeneralizing about objectionable Puritan characteristics by including the soft remarks of a young wife who is sympathetic with Hester's suffering. This expression of sympathy is in sharp contrast with the comments of the majority.[11] Another example becomes evident when Hawthorne allows Hester Prynne to remain in the community where she has committed her sins. He gives her words, actions, and thoughts that sustain her in our minds and hearts, in spite of her sins.[12]

Hawthorne's life was unhappy and insecure. He pours these feelings out in his novels, expressing his concern for the evils that dwell in the judgment of those whose duty it is to judge. Along with our discovery of his powerful techniques in imagery and symbols, we see through the tale, getting a behind-the-scenes picture of the unhappy experiences of this writer.

The following excerpt from *The Scarlet Letter* shows how the tone reveals Hawthorne's identification with the character, Hester Prynne.

When the young woman—the mother of this child—stood fully revealed before the crowd, it seemed to be her first impulse to clasp the infant closely to her bosom; not so much by an impulse of motherly affection, as that she might thereby conceal a certain token, which was wrought or fastened into her dress. In a moment, however, wisely judging that one token of her shame would poorly serve to hide another, she took the baby on her arm, and, with a burning blush, and yet a haughty smile, and a glance that would not be abashed, looked around at her townspeople and neighbors. On the breast of her gown, in the fine red cloth surrounded with an elaborate embroidery and fantastic flourishes of gold thread, appeared the scarlet letter.

Here are some of the townspeople's reaction to Hester's appearance:

"She hath good skill at her needle, that's certain," remarked one of the female spectators; "but did ever a woman, before this brazen hussy, contrive such a way of showing it! Why gossips, what is it but to laugh in the faces of our godly magistrates, and make a pride out of what they, worthy gentlemen, meant for a punishment?"

"It were well," muttered the most iron-willed of the old dames, "if we stripped Madam Hester's rich gown off her dainty shoulders, and as for the red letter, which she hath stitched so curiously, I'll bestow a rag of mine own rheumatic flannel, to make a fitter one!"

Read the excerpt a couple of times aloud. Then read the excerpt taken from Cooper's novel, *The Pilot.* You will probably agree that both authors have rendered readable stories, but readability is only one requirement of a good style. What about the language? The dialogue? Now, try to picture each setting in your mind's eye. Which excerpt has produced more lasting images?

Hawthorne and Cooper include sentences that are too long, especially for less experienced readers; still, Hawthorne's sentences are rich with an indelible imagery that the reader will find etched in his memory for a long time afterwards. Also, we do not have to go back often to reread his passages for their content. Why?

Hawthorne maintained control of the details he supplied his readers. He had the greatest devotion to his craft, writing in bold, yet poetic rhythms like a man confident in his command of the English language. Cooper wrote to entertain his readers. Although he did that, his longer descriptive passages went out of control. Action stopped while digressing descriptions rained upon the reader, erasing much of the relevant images the reader might have formed.

Hawthorne's tastes, feelings, and poetic imagery were influenced by his education, background, and writing experience. His skillfully patterned stories, which are rich in symbolic references, characterizations, settings, and theme, originate from the author's explorations into the "mysteries and trials of the human heart and soul."

Changing Tastes—Changing Styles

Readers' tastes do change with time; not to say that people like to read different *kinds* of books today than they did in the nineteenth century of Cooper and Hawthorne; but only that writing styles have changed. When we analyze nineteenth-century authors and their works, we must be careful in using the critical gauge shaped by twentieth-century tastes. Readers of the past cannot speak up in defense of their tastes in reading fare. The requirements for meeting reading interests in the past were shaped to fit the lifestyles of the period. Authors today shape their writing to fit the lifestyles and reading tastes of this end of the twentieth century.

The difference in styles between the works of the nineteeth and twentieth centuries is analogous to their differing systems of transportation: the horse and buggy versus the fast jets that crowd our airways, bringing every corner of the world closer together. Current lifestyles are charged with action, dealing with a multitude of modern inventions and institutions not dreamed of in the nineteenth century. Readers of the twentieth century demand faster paced, mainstream topics that fit with the concerns and the needs of knowledgeable, more sophisticated people.

Again, the major differences in the writing styles of the two periods lie in *how* the writers choose to tell their stories—the very heart of what style is all about.

A Modern Style in Contrast

Now we'll examine an excerpt from a more recent novel written by one of the world's most successful authors. Louis L'Amour's ninety or more novels have sold over a million copies each. Our selection is taken from the opening of *The Last of the Breed*. As you read the opener, you will notice how quickly Major Makatozi becomes a character with whom we can easily identify.

> Major Joe Makatozi stepped into the sunlight of a late afternoon. The first thing he must remember was the length of the days at this latitude. His eyes moved left and right.
>
> *About three hundred yards long, a hundred yards wide, three guard towers to a side, two men in each. A mounted*

machine gun in each tower. Each man armed with a submachine gun.

He walked behind Lieutenant Suvarov, and two armed guards followed him.

Five barracklike frame buildings, another under construction, prisoners in four of the five buildings but not all the cells occupied.

He had no illusions. He was a prisoner, and when they had extracted the information they knew he possessed, he would be killed. There was a cool freshness in the air like that from the sea, but he was far from any ocean. His first impression was, he believed, the right one. He was in the vicinity of Lake Baikal, in Siberia.

A white line six feet inside the barbed wire, the limit of approach for prisoners. The fence itself was ten feet high, twenty strands of tightly drawn, electrified wire. From the barbed wire to the edge of the forest, perhaps fifty yards.

No one knew he was alive but his captors. There would be no inquiries, no diplomatic feelers. Whatever happened now must be of his own doing. He had one asset. They had no idea what manner of man they had taken prisoner. (Louis L'Amour, *The Last of the Breed,* Bantam, 1986, pp. 4-5. Used with the permission of the publisher)

Plot: Major Joe Makatozi is being escorted from his prison cell for questioning. He observes the barbed wire and the towers with their Russian guards. He decides he is being held in Siberia, near Lake Baikal.

Conflict: "No one knew he was alive but his captors." This statement intensifies the conflict in the major's present situation and promises continued conflict throughout the novel. They can do anything to him and no one who might have acted in his behalf will know what has happened. The reader's attention is immediately caught and sustained by other details, which foreshadow a change in his situation.

Foreshadowing: "Whatever happened now must be of his own doing. He had one asset. They had no idea what manner of man they had taken prisoner." The reader is encouraged to read on and discover what manner of man the major actually is and what he will choose to do.

Atmosphere: We are able to visualize the prison yard, to follow the major's eyes as he studies the barbed wire enclosure. He is planning to escape, and we anticipate something unusual about his character and experience that will offer continued excitement as the plot unravels at a good pace.

Style: Easy to read aloud. Details laid down in unburdensome doses, providing Who, Where, and What. The answers to Why and How will come soon, as the pace gathers and holds good momentum. Sentences are varied in length and in their openings, supplying transitional space order, time order, and an order of importance that help us visualize the sequence and location of details as the story develops in a single page. We anticipate that the interrogation which is about to take place will reveal answers to our immediate questions.

By the end of the first chapter, we learn who has become the chief antagonist and what makes this character a worthy opponent for our Major Makatozi. This tantalizing information, coming in small but skillfully paced doses, builds reader interest for the next chapter and the next.

We have seen how knowledge, experience, interests, and background influence the way a story will be written. How a writer chooses to tell the story becomes a matter of style. How the public responds to that style will determine how successful the author will become.

Glossary of Prose Fiction Terms

Mastering the terminology of prose fiction is an essential task for the story analyst. Most of the following terms have been used several times throughout this book. Each is defined to fit closely with the meaning used in the text.

allegory: A story having spiritual and/or symbolic references that provide a moral; a parable

allusions: A reference to a person, thing, event, situation, real or fictional, past or present

analysis: An evaluation of any portion of a story's structural composition and of its effectiveness

antagonist: Anyone or anything presenting a challenge for the protagonist

atmosphere: Sensory descriptions of the action, the mood, and the setting

autobiographical novel: A novel that depends heavily upon the actual experiences of the author and others he knows

category novel: One of several types—mystery, detective, science fiction, gothic romances, etc.

character: What a person or thing reveals himself to be—sleazy, stealthy, humble, generous, etc.

character incident: A situation or event expressly included to characterize one or more story figures

characterization: Showing what a character is like, physically, emotionally, and intellectually

climax: High point of the story; a turning point; a showdown

commentaries: Explanatory notes used by researchers to clarify and enlighten us with what they uncover in their analyses

concepts: Thoughts; notions; something conceived in the mind concerning the nature, the purpose, and the significance of things or ideas

counterpoint: A technique that patterns diverging story threads, producing an interaction of either contrast or harmony

conflict: Problem; resistance; competition

contrasts: Opposing characteristics or interests

critical vocabulary: Words or phrases used to identify or explain the functions of a story element or a fiction writing technique

dialogues: Conversations set off by quotation marks

direct transition: The smooth unfolding of the plot, using connectives that provide details of time, space and importance, and a number of thought relationships that can be introduced in sentences

dissect: Taking the story apart to determine how each part is constructed and how each contributes to the success of the whole

dominant element: An element that is emphasized more than others in telling a story

drama of consciousness: Story where characters undergo a change in attitude concerning what is important within, among, or beyond themselves; one espousing changes in values, which emerges as a strong thematic statement

dramatic irony: When the reader becomes aware of irony in a situation, while some characters involved do not perceive what is happening to or around them

element: Either of several writing tools an author uses to create a story: character, conflict, plot, etc.

episode: A segment of a novel that includes the specific incidents that comprise one major development of a character's quest; frames the full extent of a short story

episodic conflict: Problems presented in a single episode

essential setting: A setting that is unique; the story could not have happened anywhere else

excerpt: A portion of a printed text, extracted and used for some purpose

external conflict: Problems developing around characters, motivating them to act or react in a certain way

fable: A story written expressly to teach a lesson or moral

fantasy: A story presenting an unreal world of characters, settings, and situations

fiction: Stories that are imagined

fictional genres: Specific forms of fiction: short stories and novels (prose fiction); fables, myths, plays, etc.

fiction technique: A method of developing any part of the story's structure and effects—flashbacks, symbols, propaganda, counterpoint, narrative hook, dialogue, etc.

first person POV: First person, the "I," is telling the story; we learn eveything through his eyes and through his thoughts; can be a major or minor character

flashback: Stopping the forward movement of the plot and taking readers back to a previous time

foil: A subordinate character whose sharp contrasts bring out the worst or the best in a principal character

foreshadowing: A hint of things to come, planted to arouse suspense or to heighten the reader's interest in the plot

formula story: One that follows a prescribed pattern that conforms to publishers' guidelines; certain categories of fiction—westerns, mysteries, and gothic romances—have stricter plot guidelines

genre: A specific form or class of fiction or nonfiction; short stories and novels are prose fiction genres; a biography is a genre of nonfiction

gothic novel: A romance novel usually told from a woman's viewpoint; the woman is usually caught in a stressful situation involving two men—one evil, one good, both mysterious

hero/heroine: Protagonist whose life and property are threatened by a villain

historical setting: Scenes from the past that include descriptive details of events, dress, and lifestyles appropriate to the time and place

human interest stories: Stories that hold a universal appeal; stories that tug at the heart strings

identification: Reader taking sides with the protagonist and wishing him well; observing something of ourselves in fictional characters

imagery: The mental pictures formed from details or ideas presented in speech or in description

implications: What is implied or inferred from what the author has written; what we learn by reading between the lines

incident: A happening used to characterize individuals, to clear up confusion, to provide conflict, or for other purposes indirect transition: When transition is introduced by using synonyms for words rather than repeat words in a paragraph or theme; may also be introduced by using several repetitions of words and phrases to create emphasis

insight: An ability to discern the true nature of things or situations

internal conflict: A character struggles with his conscience

internal motivation: A character acts or reacts according to his conscience

interpretive stories: Stories that supply details and ideas that leave their purposes and meanings for readers to identify and think about

irony: An element revealing the opposite of what is expected

kinetic character: A principal character who undergoes change; in the romance category, principal characters remain static, or unchanged

limited omniscient POV: A third person storyteller who can read the mind of only one character, but reports all he may perceive of any characters and setting

localized setting: One that takes us to interesting, unique places: Siberian tundra, a New England fishing village, the French Riviera

mainstream novel: One that interests readers of almost all category markets; novels with current popular themes

major crisis: Stems from an unsolved minor crisis; greater complications emerge

minor crisis: A significant problem faced by the protagonist in a short story or novel; any problem in an episode that will generate a major crisis if unsolved

monologue: A dramatic performance by only one speaker whose speech apprises us of what has been said or of what has been observed about others before or during the speech

narration: The telling of a story
narrative: A story
narrative hook: A statement or idea planted in the opening of the story and referred to several times during the length of the story; a detail from which conflict, theme, and reader identification are tapped, providing emotional effects and unifying the plot
narrator: The storyteller
naturalism: A kind of realism that probes deeply into soiled details and motives; often becomes coarse and offensive
novel: A book of fiction
novelette: A short novel
obligatory incident: An incident included to clear up confusion
out-of-character: A character acts, speaks, or thinks in a manner that conflicts with previous characterizations of him/her
pace: How slow or how fast the plot moves
parable: Stories that teach a lesson or moral; an allegory
paraphrasing: Rewriting what someone else has written; putting another's ideas into your own words
patterns: Plots; arrangement of events and the selection of specific structural elements for telling the story
perceptions: What can be experienced through our five senses
plot: Sequence of events introduced in special patterns to complete a story
plot incident: A happening that advances or thickens the plot
point-of-view: A position from which something or someone is viewed; viewpoint
POV: The abbreviation for point-of-view
principal character: The protagonist; the hero or heroine; the antagonist; the villain

propaganda: Work designed to convince others of something, without telling them why you want them to believe it

prose fiction: Fiction comprised of two genres—short stories and novels

protagonist: The principal character; may be static or kinetic

realism: Fiction that comes close to telling how life is or was in a specific time and place

resolution: The ending; problems are usually solved in a win, lose, or draw situation

resolving device: A technique that uses symbols or some other device to shed light on a major crisis and to pave the way for its resolution

romance: A class of fiction where all plot elements are idealized; characters remain unchanged

satire: Work that puts an individual or group in a ridiculous situation to usually draw attention to political, economic, or social problems

scenic setting: Brief descriptions of a place and time interwoven with the action

sentimentalism: A disposition governed or marked by strong feelings, sensibilities, or emotional idealism rather than reasoning or thought

setting: A time and place

setting incident: A situation introduced to present a time and place that is significant for telling the story

short story: A story that is short and presents a single effect

situation irony: Unexpected twists bring changes for better or for worse.

space order: Detailed descriptions that allow us to follow the action as the narrator's lens moves from one point to another within the setting

static character: Subordinate characters in most fiction; major characters are static in the romance novel

stereotypes: Characters who are presented for minor parts: police, doctors, etc.; some major characters who have not been fully developed

stream-of-consciousness: A pattern woven with a free spirit as the narrator moves from one point to another within a setting, describing anything, everything the senses may perceive at any given moment until the story ends

style: How writers express themselves

subordinate character: Minor characters; extras; static characters

subplot: Events woven in a parallel fashion to blend, eventually, with the main plot, heightening the depth and breadth of the main story

supernatural: Of or pertaining to God or a spirit or devil

suspense: Tension produced when events make us fear for the safety or success of our protagonist

symbol: Anything used to represent something else—a nation's flag, a rattlesnake, etc.

symbolic setting: Setting that stands for some key element in the plot; one that foreshadows what is going to happen—a story, a full moon, ominous clouds

technique: A unique way of doing anything

theme: The underlying idea; the moral; the lesson learned

third person objective POV: Third person reports only what he sees and hears; he becomes the readers' eyes and ears

third person omniscient POV: Third person narrator knows and reports all; he enters the minds of all characters, reporting their thoughts and conversations at various times

time order: Arrangement of details to keep us aware of the passage of time, including stopping of time to add a flashback

transition: A method for taking the reader from scene to scene, from present to past action and back again without confusing the reader

verbal irony: Characters mean the opposite of what they say.

viewpoint: The eyes through which the story is being seen and told; a point from which the narrator makes his observations

villain: The person or thing that threatens to destroy the life and property of the hero and/or heroine

visualization: The ability to form mental pictures from the details of setting and action supplied by the writer

Notes

Chapter 1

1. Stephen J. Wagner, an excerpt from "Fabulous Fictions," in "The Writing Life," *Writer's Digest,* February 1987, p. 6.

Chapter 2

1. Bruce R. McElderry, Jr., *Thomas Wolfe* (New York: Twayne Publishers, Inc., 1984), pp. 89, 90.
2. Dick Perry, *One Way to Write Your Novel* (1969; reprint, Cincinnati: Writer's Digest Books, 1983), p. 75.
3. Lawrence Block, "Why Write A Novel?" in *Writing the Novel from Plot to Print* (Cincinnati: Writer's Digest Books, 1983), pp. 20, 21.
4. Ibid.
5. Ibid.
6. Laurence Perrine, ed., *Literature: Structure, Sound, and Sense* (New York: Harcourt, Brace, and World, Inc., 1970), p. 4.
7. Ibid.

Chapter 3

1. Anne Gisconny, "Formulas for Writing the Romantic Novel," in *How to Write a Romance* by Katherine Falk, reprinted in *1983-84 Fiction Writer's Market* (Cincinnati: Writer's Digest Books, 1983) with the permission of Denise Marcil Agency, p. 196.
2. Stephen J. Wagner, "The Writing Life," p. 6.
3. Ibid.
4. Ibid.
5. W. A. Craik, *The Brontë Novels* (New York: Methuen & Co. Ltd., 1968), p. 196.
6. Ibid., p. 7-9.
7. Ibid., p. 71.
8. Warren French, *John Steinbeck* (Boston: Twayne Publishers, 1975), p. 170.
9. Ibid., pp. 95-99.
10. Ibid.
11. Ibid.
12. Robert B. Downs, "Afterword" to *The Jungle*, by Upton Sinclair (New York: NAL, Inc., 1960), pp. 345-349.

Chapter 4

1. Les Boston, "The Right Viewpoint: How to Choose and Use Point of View Effectively," in *1983-84 Fiction Writer's Market*, p. 140.
2. Orson Scott Card, "The Finer Points of Characterization, Part I," *Writer's Digest*, October 1987, p. 27.
3. Ibid.
4. Ibid., p. 28.
5. Conrad Richter, *The Light in the Forest* (New York: Alfred A. Knopf, Inc., 1966; reprinted in Bantam Paperback Edition, 1984), p. 45.
6. Ibid.
7. Elizabeth Scheld, ed., *Designs in Fiction* (New York: The Macmillan Company, 1968), pp. 4, 43, 132.

Chapter 5

1. Orson Scott Card, "The Finer Points of Characterization, Part III," *Writer's Digest,* December, 1986, p. 32.
2. Ibid.
3. Ibid.
4. Rega Kramer McCarty, "Using Symbols as a Shortcut to Meaning," WDS Forum March/April 1981; reprinted in *1983-84 Fiction Writer's Market* (Cincinnati: Writer's Digest Books, 1983), p. 145.
5. Allan Glatthorn, Richard S. Hartman, and C. F. Main, *The Student's Guide to Ideas and Patterns in Literature II,* teacher's edition (New York: Harcourt Brace Jovanovich, Inc., 1970), pp. 2-4, 6-8.
6. Ibid.
7. Eva Fitzwater, ed., Cliff Notes to John Steinbeck's *The Pearl* (Lincoln: Cliff Notes, Inc., 1966), pp. 10, 11, 46, 52.
8. Ibid., pp. 44, 46, 47.

Chapter 6

1. Les Boston, "The Right Viewpoint," p. 139.
2. Ibid., p. 136.
3. Ibid., pp. 138-143.
4. Lawrence Block, *Writing the Novel,* p. 149.
5. Ibid.
6. Les Boston, "The Right Viewpoint," pp. 138, 139.
7. Ibid., p. 140.
8. Ibid., pp. 140, 141.
9. Ibid.
10. Stanley J. Kunitz and Vineta Colby, eds., *European Authors 1000-1900* (New York: The H. W. Wilson Company, 1967), pp. 614, 615.
11. Damon Knight, "Keeping Readers on Their Toes," *Writer's Digest,* March 1988, p. 38.

12. Ibid.
13. Ibid.
14. Lawrence Block, *Writing the Novel,* p. 150.
15. Ibid., p. 151.
16. Ibid.
17. Ibid.
18. Jean Z. Owen, *Professional Fiction Writing* (Boston: The Writer, Inc.,1974), p. 47.
19. Ibid.
20. Ibid., p. 46.

Chapter 7

1. Orson Scott Card, "The Finer Points of Characterization, Part III," p. 32.
2. Ibid.
3. Diane Doubtfire, "Creating Imaginary Characters," *1983-84 Fiction Writer's Market,* p. 109.
4. Randall Boyll, "When They Cry It Makes Me Happy," *Writer's Digest,* May 1987, p. 24.
5. Ibid.
6. Diane Doubtfire, "Creating Imaginary Characters," p. 108.
7. Ibid.
8. Ralph Boas and Edwin Smith, "What to Consider in Studying Characters," in *Enjoyment of Literature* (New York: Harcourt Brace & Company, 1934), pp. 214-216. Though this volume is dated, it remains a treasury of resources for all phases of fiction writing, analyzing both short stories and novels that have become classics the world over. Studies in poetry appreciation should also prove helpful for young writers interested in writing and publishing their poetry.
9. Ibid.
10. Esther M. Friesner, "Now What Do We Do With the Alligators?" *Writer's Digest,* January 1988, p. 34.

11. Ibid.
12. Ibid.
13. Ibid.

Chapter 8

1. Ralph Boas and Edwin Smith, *Enjoyment of Literature*, pp. 219, 220.
2. Ibid.
3. Orson Scott Card, "The Finer Points of Characterization, Part III," p. 87.
4. Ralph Boas and Edwin Smith, *Enjoyment of Literature*, p. 219.
5. Stephen J. Wagner, "The Writing Life," p. 6.

Chapter 9

1. Phyllis A. Whitney, *Guide To Fiction Writing* (Boston: The Writer, 1982), pp. 105, 106.
2. Jean Z. Owen, *Professional Fiction Writing*, p. 110.
3. Ibid., pp. 113, 114.
4. Ralph Boas and Edwin Smith, *Enjoyment of Literature*, p. 231.
5. Ibid.
6. Ibid.
7. Phyllis A. Whitney, *Guide to Fiction Writing*, p. 85.

Chapter 10

1. Eudora Welty, "Some Notes on Time in Fiction," in *The Eye of the Needle*, reprinted in *1983-84 Fiction Writer's Market*, p. 102.
2. Ibid., p. 103.
3. Phyllis Whitney, *Guide to Fiction Writing*, p. 113.
4. Ibid., p. 114.
5. Ibid.
6. Ibid.

Chapter 11

1. F. A. Rockwell, "Start with Clashing Goals," in *How To Write Plots That Sell,* reprinted in *1983-84 Fiction Writer's Market,* p. 129.
2. James McKimmey, "All's Well That Ends Well," in *1983-84 Fiction Writer's Market,* p. 156.
3. Ibid.
4. Ibid.
5. F. A. Rockwell, "Start with Clashing Goals," p. 126.
6. Phyllis Whitney, *Guide to Fiction Writing,* p. 63.
7. Ibid., p. 64.
8. Dean R. Koontz, "Why Novels of Fear Must Do More Than Frighten," in *How to Write Tales of Horror, Fantasy & Science Fiction,* ed. J. N. Williamson (Cincinnati: Writer's Digest Books, 1983), p. 103.
9. Phyllis Whitney, *Guide to Fiction Writing,* p. 98.
10. Ibid.
11. Dean Koontz, "Why Novels of Fear," p. 103.
12. F. A. Rockwell, "Start with Clashing Goals," p. 128.
13. Liam O'Flaherty, "The Sniper," in *Designs in Fiction,* edited with commentary, by Elizabeth Scheld (New York: The MacMillan Company, 1968), p. 19.

Chapter 12

1. Jean Z. Owen, *Professional Fiction Writing,* p. 24.
2. Ibid., p. 26.
3. Laurence Perrine, ed., *Literature: Structure, Sound, and Sense,* p. 100.
4. Ibid., p. 106.
5. Jean Z. Owen, *Professional Fiction Writing,* pp. 26, 27.
6. R. W. Stallman, "Notes toward an Analysis of The Red Badge of Courage," in *The Norton Critical Edition of The Red Badge of*

Courage, eds. Scully Bradly, Richmond Croom Beatty, and E. Hudson Long (New York: W. W. Norton Company, Inc., 1962), p. 251.

7. Ibid., p. 252.
8. Ibid., p. 251.
9. Robert B. Downs, "Afterword" to *The Jungle*, p. 349.
10. Herman Melville, from film summary of "Bartleby," appearing in *Short Story Showcase*, a guide published by South Carolina ETV Network, revised edition, June 1981, p. 16.
11. Ibid.
12. Ibid.

Chapter 13

1. Isaac Asimov, "Introduction" to *Short Science Fiction Tales*. (New York: Crowell-Collier, 1963); reprinted. (London: Collier Books, Collier-Macmillan Ltd., 1970), p. 12.
2. Ibid.
3. Ibid.
4. Terms were drawn from Boas and Smith, Chapter 13, "How to Study Story Building," in *Enjoyment of Literature*, pp. 200-202.
5. Lawrence Block, "Fifteen Things You Must Know About Writing the Short Story," *Writer's Digest*, July 1988, p. 28.
6. Edward Hoch, "Open and Shut Cases:Writing Beginnings and Endings in Fiction," *Writer's Digest*, September 1986, pp. 39, 40.
7. Ibid.

Chapter 14

1. G. Robert Carlson, comp., *Encounters* (New York: Webster Division, McGraw-Hill Book Company, 1973), pp. 503, 504.
2. Laurence Perrine, ed., *Literature: Structure, Sound, and Sense*, pp. 4, 5.
3. Ibid.
4. Ibid., p. 228.

5. G. Robert Carlson, comp., *Western Literature* (New York: Webster Division, McGraw-Hill, Inc., 1973), p. 689.
6. Lawrence Block, "Writing the Short Story," pp. 27, 28.
7. Ibid.

Chapter 15

1. Boas and Smith, *Enjoyment of Literature,* pp. 193-196.
2. Ibid. p. 137.
3. Louise Bogan and Josephine Schaefer, "Afterword" to *A Writer's Diary,* by Virginia Woolf, ed. Leonard Woolf (New York: Harcourt, Brace & World, 1954; reprint, NAL, Inc., Signet Classic edition, 1968), pp. 343.

Chapter 16

1. Boas and Smith, *Enjoyment of Literature,* p. 197.
2. Ibid.
3. Ibid.
4. Phyllis Whitney, *Guide to Fiction Writing,* p. 83.
5. Ibid.
6. Ibid., p. 84.
7. Lawrence Block, *Writing the Novel,* p. 8.
8. Ibid.

Chapter 17

1. Rega Kramer McCarty, "Using Symbols as a Shortcut to Meaning," p. 147.
2. Ibid., pp. 145, 146. Purposes for symbols were drawn from this chapter and have been paraphrased. Illustrations for these have been taken from applications in a variety of other stories, and these sources are noted in the text.
3. Ibid. p. 146.
4. Philip Rahv, from "The Symbolic Fallacy in Crane Criticism,"

in *Kenyon Review* 18 (Spring 1956), pp. 276-287, passim; reprinted in *The Norton Critical Edition, The Red Badge of Courage*, eds. Scully Bradly, Richard Croom Beatty, and E. Hudson Long (New York: W. W. Norton Company, Inc., 1962), pp. 289-291.

5. Rega Kramer McCarty, "Using Symbols as a Shortcut to Meaning," p. 147.

Chapter 18

1. Dick Perry, *One Way to Write Your Novel*, p. 26.
2. Jean Z. Owen, *Professional Fiction Writing*, p. 99.
3. Hal Blythe and Charlie Sweet, "Taking Care of Business," *Writer's Digest*, February 1987, p. 40.

Chapter 19

1. Mariana Prieto, "What You Should Know about Using the Flashback," (F & W Publishing Co., 1967); reprinted in *The Writer's Digest Handbook of Short Story Writing*, eds. Frank A. Dickson and Sandra Smythe (Cincinnati: Writer's Digest Books, 1981), p. 160.
2. Susan Thaler, "How to Use the Flashback in Fiction," Dickson and Smythe, eds., *Writer's Digest Handbook*, p. 155.
3. Mariana Prieto, "Using the Flashback," p. 161.
4. James Leo Herlihy, *Midnight Cowboy* (New York: Simon and Schuster, 1965), pp. 18, 19.
5. Mariana Prieto, "Using the Flashback," p. 161.

Chapter 21

1. Val Thiessen, "Five Suggestions for Writing Transitions," (F & W Publishing Co., 1963); reprinted in Dickson and Smythe, eds., *Writer's Digest Handbook*, p. 169.
2. Ibid., pp. 168, 169.
3. Robert C. Meridith and John D. Fitzgerald, "Transitions," in

The Professional Story Writer and His Art (New York: Thomas Y. Crowel, 1963); reprinted in Dickson and Smythe eds. *Writer's Digest Handbook,* p. 148.

4. Val Thiessen, "Five Suggestions for Writing Transitions," p. 168.

5. Louise Boggess, "How to Choose the Right Viewpoint for Your Story," in Dickson and Smythe, eds., *Writer's Digest Handbook,* p. 148.

Chapter 22

1. John A. Garraty and Jerome L. Sternstein, "James Fenimore Cooper," in *Encyclopedia of American Biography* (New York: Harper & Row, Publishers, 1974), pp. 221-223.
2. Ibid.
3. Lawrence Block, "Staying Loose," *Writer's Digest,* November 1986, pp. 58, 59.
4. Hallie and Whit Burnett, "The Manner of the Telling," *1983-84 Fiction Writer's Market,* p. 149.
5. Ibid.
6. Dick Perry, *One Way to Write Your Novel,* p. 46.
7. Lawrence Block, *Writing the Novel,* p. 11.
8. Hallie and Whit Burnett, "The Manner of the Telling," p. 149.
9. Lawrence Block, *Writing the Novel,* p. 11.
10. G. Robert Carlson, comp., *American Literature: Themes and Writers* (New York: McGraw-Hill, Inc., 1973), pp. 67-70.
11. Paul R. Stewart, "Introduction" to Nathaniel Hawthorne's *The Scarlet Letter* (Lincoln: Cliff Notes, Inc., 1960), p. 6.
12. G. Robert Carlson, comp., *American Literature,* pp. 9-12.

Bibliography

Nonfiction

Asimov, Isaac. "Introduction" to *Short Science Fiction Tales.* London: Collier-Macmillan, 1970.

Block, Lawrence. *Writing the Novel from Plot to Print.* Cincinnati: Writer's Digest Books, 1983.

———. "Staying Loose." *Writer's Digest.* November 1986.

———. "Fifteen Things You Must Know About Writing the Short Story." *Writer's Digest.* July 1988.

Blythe, Hal, and Sweet, Charlie. "Taking Care of Business." *Writer's Digest,* February 1987.

Boyll, Randall. "When They Cry It Makes Me Happy." *Writer's Digest.* May 1987.

Bradly, Scully, Richard Croom Beaty, and E. Hudson Long, eds. *The Norton Critical Edition of The Red Badge of Courage.* New York: W. W. Norton & Company, Inc., 1962.

Card, Orson Scott. "The Finer Points of Characterization, Parts I and III." *Writer's Digest.* December 1986.

Carlson, G. Robert, ed. *Encounters.* New York: Webster Division, McGraw Hill Book Co., 1973.

Craik, W. A. *The Brontë Novels.* London: Methuen & Co. Ltd., 1968.

Dickson, Frank A., and Sandra Smythe, eds. *The Writer's Digest Handbook of Short Story Writing.* Cincinnati: Writer's Digest Books, 1981.

Downs, Robert B. "Afterword" to *The Jungle,* by Upton Sinclair. New York: NAL, Signet Edition, 1960.

Fitzwater, Eva. commentary to *The Pearl,* by John Steinbeck. Lincoln: Cliff's Notes, 1966.

Fredette, Jean M., ed. *1983-84 Fiction Writer's Market.* Cincinnati: Writer's Digest Books, 1983.

French, Warren. *John Steinbeck.* Boston: Twayne Publishers, 1975.

Friesner, Esther M. "Now What Do You Do with the Alligators?" *Writer's Digest.* January 1988.

Garraty, John A. and Jerome L. Sternstein, eds. *Encyclopedia of American Biography.* New York: Harper & Row, Publishers, 1974.

Glatthorn, Allen, Richard S.Hartman, and C. F. Main, eds. *The Student's Guide to Ideas and Patterns in Literature II.* Teacher's edition. New York: Harcourt, Brace Jovanovich, 1970.

Hoch, Edward D. "Open and Shut Cases: Writing Beginnings and Endings in Fiction." *Writer's Digest.* September 1986.

Knight, Damon. "Keeping Readers on Their Toes." *Writer's Digest.* March 1988.

Kunitz, Stanley J. and Vineta Colby, eds. *European Authors 1000-1900.* New York: The H. W. Wilson Co., 1967.

Kunitz, Stanley J. and Howard Haycroft, eds. *American Authors.* New York: H. W. Wilson Company, 1949.

McElderry, Bruce R. *Thomas Wolfe.* New York: Twayne Publishers, 1984.

Melville, Herman. "Bartleby." Film summary in *Short Story Showcase.* Columbia, South Carolina, ETV Network Guide, June 1981.

Owen, Jean Z. *Professional Fiction Writing.* Boston: The Writer, Inc., 1974.

Perrine, Laurence, ed. *Literature: Structure, Sound, and Sense.* New York: Harcourt, Brace, and World, Inc., 1970.

Perry, Dick. *One Way to Write a Novel.* Cincinnati: Writer's Digest Books, 1983.

Polking, Kirk. *A Beginner's Guide to Getting Published.* Cincinnati: Writer's Digest Books, 1987.

Scheld, Elizabeth, ed. *Designs in Fiction.* New York: The Macmillan Company, 1968.

Wagner, Stephen J. "The Writing Life." *Writer's Digest,* February, 1987.

Whitney, Phyllis A. *Guide to Fiction Writing.* Boston: The Writer, Inc., 1982.

Williamson, J. W., ed. *How to Write Tales of Horror, Fantasy & Science Fiction.* Cincinnati: Writer's Digest Books, 1983.

Woolf, Leonard. ed. *A Writer's Diary by Virginia Woolf.* New York: Harcourt, Brace & World, Inc., 1954; reprint, New York: NAL, Inc., 1968.

Fiction

Brontë, Charlotte. *Jane Eyre.* New York: John C. Winston Company, 1954.

Brontë, Emily. *Wuthering Heights.* New York: Random House Publishers, 1943.

Clavel, James. *Shogun, A Novel of Japan.* 2 vols. New York: Atheneum, 1975.

Cooper, James Fenimore. *The Pilot.* New York: Dodd, Mead & Company, 1947.

Coxe, George Harmon. *The Big Gamble.* New York: Alfred A. Knopf, 1958.

Crane, Stephen. *The Red Badge of Courage, A Norton Critical Edition.* New York: W. W. Norton Company, Inc., 1962.

Fitzgerald, F. Scott. *The Great Gatsby.* New York: Charles Scribner's Sons, 1931, 1961.

Franco, Marjorie. "A Chance of a Lifetime." *Redbook,* March 1989.

Galsworthy, John. "The Japanese Quince," in *Caravan.* London: William Heinemann, Ltd., 1910. Reprinted in *Literature:*

Structure, Sound, and Sense, edited by Laurence Perrine. New York: Harcourt, Brace & World, 1970.

Hall, Lyn. *Gently Touch The Milkweed.* Chicago: Follet Publishing Company, 1970. Reprint, New York: Avon, 1977.

Hawthorne, Nathaniel. *The Scarlet Letter.* New York: Washington Square Press, Inc., 1961.

Hemingway, Ernest. *Men Without Women.* New York: Charles Scribner's Sons, 1927.

Herlihy, James Leo. *Midnight Cowboy.* New York: Simon and Schuster, 1965.

Hood, Ann. "Fanning An Old Flame," *Redbook,* March 1989.

Hurst, James. "The Scarlet Ibis," *Atlantic Monthly,* July 1960.

Jackson, Shirley. "The Lottery." In *The Lottery.* New York: Farrar, Straus & Giroux, Inc., 1948.

King, Stephen. *Pet Sematery.* New York: Doubleday & Company, 1983. Reprint. Signet Edition, 1984.

L'Amour, Louis. *The Last of the Breed.* New York: Bantam Books, 1986.

Mansfield, Katherine. "Miss Brill." In *The Short Stories of Katherine Mansfield.* New York: Alfred A. Knopf, Inc., 1922.

Mitchell, Margaret. *Gone with the Wind.* Anniversary edition with introduction, by James A. Michener. New York: Macmillan Publishing Company, 1975.

Myrer, Anton. *The Last Convertible.* New York: G. Putnam's Sons, 1978.

O'Henry. *The Complete Works of O'Henry.* New York: Doubleday & Company, 1953.

Orwell, George. *Animal Farm.* Illustrated by Joey Batchelor and John Halas. New York: Harcourt, Brace & World, Inc., 1954.

Poe, Edgar Allen. *Tales and Poems of Edgar Allen Poe.* New York: Macmillan, 1973.

Reeman, Douglas. *To Risks Unknown.* 1st American ed. New York: Putnam, 1970.

Richter, Conrad. *The Light in the Forest*. New York: Alfred A. Knopf, 1966. Reprint. Bantam, 1984.

Sinclair, Upton. *The Jungle*. New York: Viking, 1946. Reprint. New American Library, 1960.

Steinbeck, John. *The Grapes of Wrath*. New York: Viking Press, 1939. Reprint. Penguin Books, 1981.

———. *The Pearl*. New York: Viking Press, Inc., 1945.

Stevenson, Robert Louis. *The Complete Short Stories of Robert Louis Stevenson*, edited with introduction. by Charles Neider. Garden City: Doubleday, 1969.

Swift, Jonathan. *Gulliver's Travels*. New York: Dell Publishing Co., Inc. Reprint. Laurel Edition, 1961.

Thurber, James. *The Thurber Carnival*. New York: Harper & Row, 1945.

Waller, Leslie. "The Restless Ones." In *Focus: Themes in Literature*, ed. G. Robert Carlsen. New York: McGraw-Hill, 1969.

Wouk, Herman. *War and Remembrance*. 2 vols. Boston: Little, Brown and Company, 1978.

Index